CAPITALS
FOR
CALLIGRAPHY

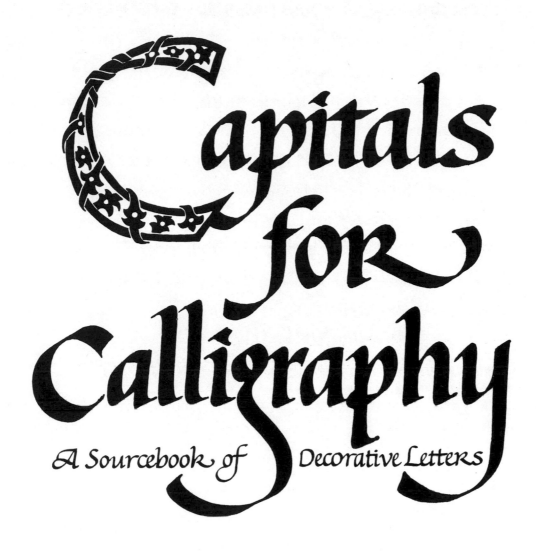

Capitals for Calligraphy

A Sourcebook of Decorative Letters

Margaret Shepherd

COLLIER BOOKS
A Division of Macmillan Publishing Co., Inc., New York

Macmillan Publishing Co., Inc.
866 Third Avenue, New York, N.Y 10022

Collier Macmillan Canada, Inc.

LIBRARY of CONGRESS CATALOGING IN PUBLICATION DATA

Shepherd, Margaret
    Capitals for calligraphy

    Includes index.
    1. Calligraphy. 2. Lettering. 3. English language — Capitalization.
4. Filigree lettering. I. Title.

Z43.5543 1981   745. 6'1   81~10169
ISBN 0~02~029960~5 (pbk)   AACR2

First Collier Books edition 1981

Fourth printing 1983

Printed in the United States of America

TABLE of CONTENTS

Acknowledgements   vi

Preface ~ Using This Book   vii

I. CHOOSING A PEN   1

II. REVIEWING THE SMALL LETTERS   13

III. 2500 YEARS OF PEN CAPITALS   25

IV. DRAWING A DECORATED INITIAL   55

V. PLACING CAPITALS ON THE PAGE   65

VI. AN ABECEDARY OF CAPITALS   81

& BIBLIOGRAPHY, GLOSSARY AND INDEX   108

ACKNOWLEDGEMENTS

I wish to thank the people who helped think up, research, and write this book and see it safely through to publication. Connie Hart gave me a book of Victorian capitals many years ago that fueled my interest in the decorative letter. Leslie Miller and Richard McElroy helped track down elusive references. Sarah Friend housed me during every last-minute deadline.

Some copyright material is included here, with grateful acknowledgement to the following sources:

26 Man holding scroll is from a kylix by Douris, and is reproduced by permission of the Staatliche Museum, Berlin.
28 Carved inscription is from the tomb of a legionary, and is reproduced by permission of the Rheinisches Landesmuseum, Bonn.
28 Logo is reproduced by permission of Advent Corporation, Cambridge, Ma.
30 Celtic lettering is from The Book of Kells, and is reproduced by permission of the Board of Trinity College, Dublin.
32 Runic lettering is from the Ardagh Chalice, and is reproduced by permission of the National Museum of Ireland.
34, 36, 40, 48, 50 Lettering and initials are from various books in the Pictorial Archive Series, Dover Publications. (82-107 initials are credited in captions.)

42 Capital 'A' is from A Renaissance Alphabet by Giovan Francesco Cresci, and is reproduced by permission of the university of Wisconsin Press, Madison. Special thanks to Donald Anderson.
44 Title page is from King Harald and the Icelanders, and is reproduced by permission of Penmaen Press.
44 Cover design is from East to America by Robert A. Wilson and Bill Hosukawa, and is reproduced by permission of William Morrow & Co.
46 Cover design is from The Lost Books of the Bible, and is reproduced by permission of Bell Publishing Co., a division of Crown Publishing, Inc.
52 Cover design is from The Snow Leopard by Peter Matthiesson, and is reproduced by permission of viking Press.

63 Photographs #1, 2, and 8 are reproduced by permission of Stanley Kugell. (Other photographs are by the author.)
85, 107 Capital 'D' and 'Z' are from Jan Tschichold: Typographer by Rauri McLean, and are reproduced by permission of David R. Godine, Publisher.
86 Capital 'E' is by Johan Steingruber, and is reproduced by permission of the Metropolitan Museum of Art, New York.
101 Capital 'J' is by Ketly Oechsli, and is reproduced by permission of the New York Times.
104 Capital 'W' is from 'Power Failures of 1976,' New York magazine, and is reproduced by permission of Robert Grossman.

In addition, David Friend and Jasper deserve my thanks for their stoicism in the face of the demands that book production makes on their daily life. They indirectly put a lot of love into this book, too.

PREFACE~USING THIS BOOK

Capital letters hold a special magic for calligrapher and reader alike. In front of a word, they confer Honor or extra emphasis. A word written in ALL CAPITALS, whether at the head of a page or buried in the text, commands attention. Adding even a small decorated initial to a block of text brings the page to life. And a large illuminated capital often conveys more information than the few lines of small letters it leaves space for. Capitals precede lowercase letters historically, and as the older image they carry more authority; throughout the Middle Ages, in fact, scribes always used newer styles for text letters & older forms for headings. Today, children learning to write learn the 2000-year-old Roman capitals first, and at an early age can distinguish between capital & small.

CAPITALS FOR CALLIGRAPHY follows the procession of capital letters over the last 25 centuries. After choosing a pen in Chapter I and reviewing the small letters in Chapter II, you will be introduced in Chapter III to 14 basic capital alphabets, designed to mark important milestones in the development of capitals and to complement your small-letter alphabets. Chapter IV, building on these pen-lettered forms, constructs and analyzes the decorated letter, showing not only how to draw it but also where to seek new ideas. Chapter V emphasizes the capital's relation to the design of the whole page. In this chapter the style of the letters and the layout of the whole page look like what the text is talking about — a quality of self-reference that is one of calligraphy's most beguiling characteristics. Finally, over 200 capital designs from diverse sources are collected in Chapter VI to show the vitality and rich variation of decorated initials.

CAPITALS FOR CALLIGRAPHY can be useful to the beginner as an introduction to history & technique, to the intermediate scribe as a methodical dissection of an otherwise sometimes overwhelming body of material, to the advanced calligrapher as a sourcebook of designs and layouts, and to the interested onlooker as a kind of map of the terrain. This book barely scratches the surface. It is meant to display the variety of capital letter design, outline some of the reasons the letters look the way they do, provide a framework for practice, and guide the reader to further reading. As with so many other aspects of the art of calligraphy, however, the letters themselves, as they take shape under your pen, are the best teachers you could possibly have.

Margaret Shepherd

Boston
1 September 1981

ME
LITTERULAS
STULTI
DOCUERE

For my parents
who foolishly taught me
to read and write.

MARTIAL · EPIGRAMS
A.D. 93

CHOOSING A PEN

Because capital letters can be either pen-lettered with a broad-edge pen or drawn with a pointed pen, the pens pictured on the following 10 pages are shown in two groups. Many broad-edge pens are sold in a range of nib widths, ink colors, & prices. Even a beginning scribe will want to own more than one: fiber-tip markers, large and small, for fool-proof practice and rough drafts; a fountain pen for handwriting and more careful practice; a dip pen for india-inked finished work. The pointed pens for drawing are borrowed from the artist and the draftsman.

Calligraphy pens, once only to be found in very specialized stores and through mail order sources, are increasingly easy to find. Start by checking at your local art, craft, office, or stationery store. Take this book with you; the addresses next to the pen illustrations will help you and the store manager to track down any pens the store does not have in stock. Patronize your store whenever possible. You can try pens before you buy; you can buy pens without delay; store personnel may be able to suggest other calligraphy-related supplies you are unacquainted with. Many of the pens shown here are also available from mail order sources, a few of which are listed on page 12.

This symbol means a pen is available in a special oblique version designed for left-handers.

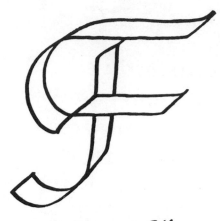

For centuries following the decline of the Roman empire, pens were made of everyday materials, shaped by the skill of the scribe to suit his lettering needs. Today, pens are still handmade by scribes for convenience, independence, elegance, and the authentic 'feel' quills give. (Avoid art-store feather pens of unreliable origin and dyed plumage; they are mainly for show.)

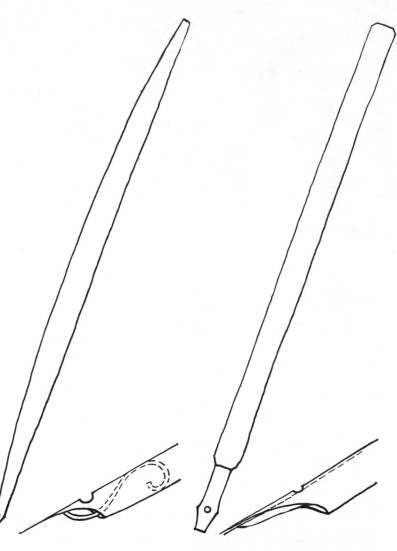

Cut to desired width from | to ▮

F1 F2 F3 M1 M2 M3 B1 B2 B3

The Society of Scribes and Illuminators keeps alive the art of quill cutting & lists reliable suppliers. SS1, 43 Earlham St, London, WC2, England

This synthetic quill-like point has a unique capillary ink feed. Dip or fountain pen. Braun Writing Instruments, 15 Georgia Dr, Syosset, N.Y. 11791

The march of progress did not bypass the calligrapher's broad-edged pen. Improved techniques of metal-working, plus increased trade and communication, brought a gradual shift from the medieval quill to the post-Renaissance metal-tipped dip pen. Contemporary calligraphers still prefer this kind of pen for its ease of use, relatively widespread availability, and uniformity.

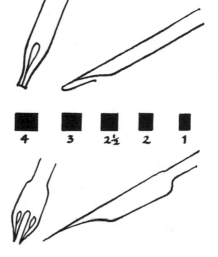

| 4 | 3 | 2½ | 2 | 1 |

| 00 | 0 | 1 | 1½ | 2 | 2½ | 3 | 3½ | 4 | 4½ | 5 | 6 |

| 10 | 20 | 30 | 40 | 50 | 60 | 80 |

The Mitchell Round-hand pen offers a built-in reservoir for less frequent ink dipping, and interchangeable nibs. Also oblique left & right.

Other Mitchell nibs include wide Witch pens & double-pointed Scroll pens. Pentalic, 132 West 22nd St, New York, N.Y. 10011 U.S. Distributor

Pelikan Graphos nibs fit an internal reservoir but, unlike true fountain pens, use India ink & need cleaning after every use.

Widths in mm ½ ¾ 1 1½ 2 2½ 3 4 5

C0 C1 C2 C3 C4 C5 C6

0.8 1 1.25 1.6 2.5 4.0 6.4 10 mm

Brause lettering nibs are somewhat stiffer than Mitchell. Each nib has a reservoir. Pentalic, 132 W. 22nd St., New York, N.Y. 10011. U.S. distributor.

Speedball nibs, in a smaller array of nibs than Mitchell & Brause, each have a reservoir. Hunt Mfg. Co., 1405 Locust Street, Philadelphia, Pa 19102

The Pelikan Graphos system lets the scribe write without re-dipping so often. Koh-I-Noor, 100 North St., Bloomsbury, N.J., 08804. U.S. distributor.

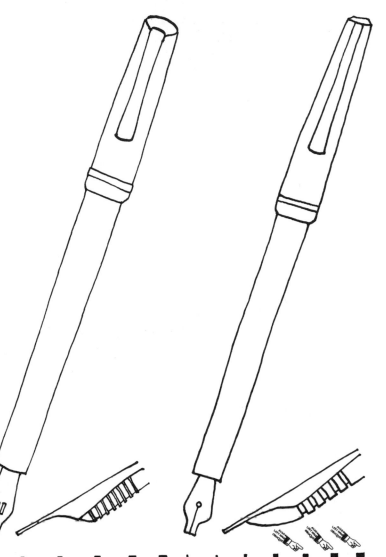

E

ngland's industrial revolution bore fruit for calligraphers with the late 19th-century invention of the fountain pen. While the point resembles a dip pen, the ink supply is held inside the pen body and fed to the nib by capillary action. Easier to handle than dip pens, fountain pens have one drawback for serious calligraphers: they use water-soluble, rather than water-proof, ink.

The Osmiroid pen has different widths for lettering and for writing. Oblique left and right. Hunt Mfg Co., 1405 Locust St., Philadelphia, Pa. 19102

similar to Osmiroid, Platignum pens offer a firm chisel-edged nib in many widths. Pentalic, 132 W. 22nd St., New York, N.Y. 10011. U.S. distributor.

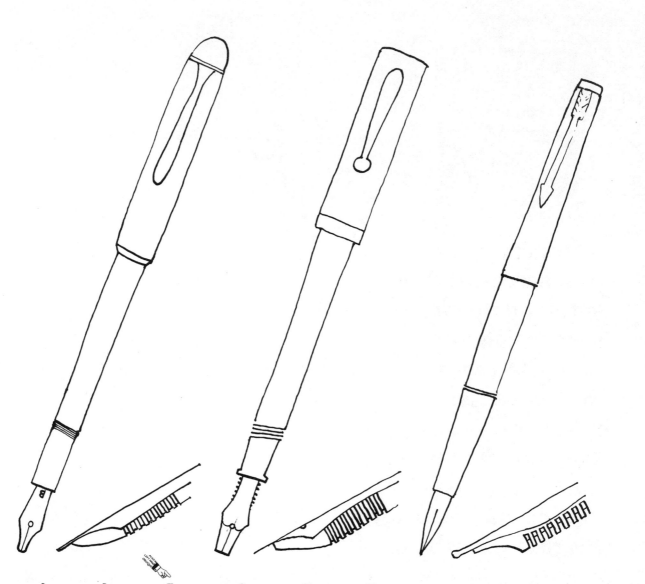

Fine   Medium   Broad   Fine   Medium   Broad

The Pelikan fountain pen, for handwriting rather than lettering, has a slightly rounded, gold-clad point. Koh-I-Noor, 100 North St, Bloomsbury, N.J. 08804

The first cartridge calligraphy pen, the Shaeffer "No-Nonsense" pen is widely available. Shaeffer, Fort Madison, Iowa 52627

The 'broad' signature nib of the Parker pen can serve as a calligraphy point. Parker Pen Co., Colvin St., Jamesville, Wis. 53545

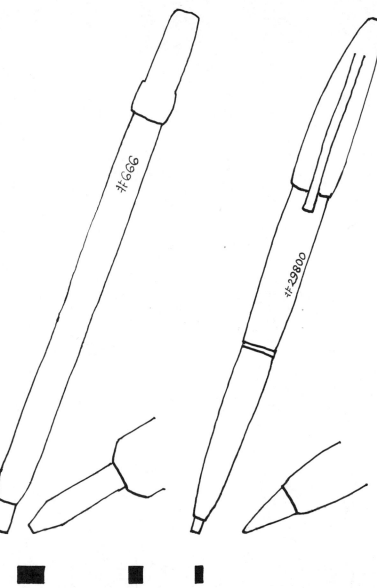

Materials technology of the 20th century first dealt calligraphy a death-blow in the form of the ballpoint pen, and then gave it a miracle cure with the invention of the chisel-tip felt pen (now no longer real felt, following the development of a stiffer and longer-lasting fiber). Available in many widths and colors, markers are idiot-proof, leak-proof, & in true 20th century style, disposable.

For large letters, the Pentalic Lettering Marker is a reliable practice pen. Water-soluble ink. 2 sizes. Pentalic, 132 W. 22nd St., New York, N.y. 10011

For small lettering & large handwriting this Calligraphic Pen has a strong nib & 5 basic colors. Sanford Corporation, Bellwood, Ill. 60104

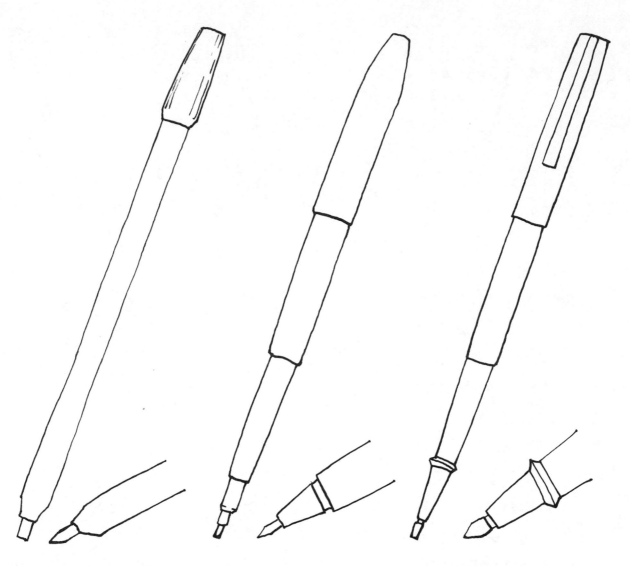

The Niji Stylist Calligraphy Marker includes a useful medium~width nib. Yasumoto & Co., 24 California St., San Francisco, Cal. 94111

The Chiz'l pen offers a wide range of subtle colors; the tip is softer and narrower than other markers. Cooper Color, 300 Mercury Rd., Jacksonville, Fla. 32207

Design Art offers the Chisel Point Marker in many bright hues and two nib widths. Eberhard Faber Crestwood, Wilkes-Barre, Pa. 18703

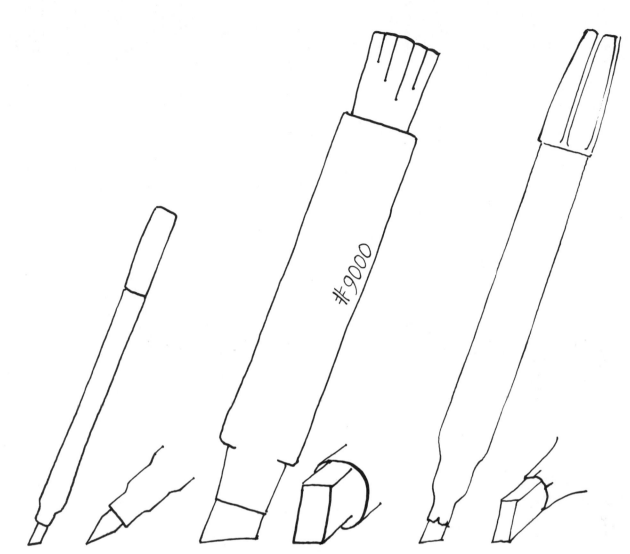

#9000

Fluorescent colors and an oblique nib characterize the diminutive Marvy marker. Uchida, 69-34 51st Avenue, Woodside, N.Y. 11377

Oblique fiber-tipped markers can be useful if the calligrapher allows for the discrepancy in the pen angle. A marker nib has 2 stroke widths.

Shown at center, the Jumbo Marvy marker (Uchida). Above, Design-Art pen. Eberhard Faber, Crestwood, Wilkes-Barre, Pa. 18703

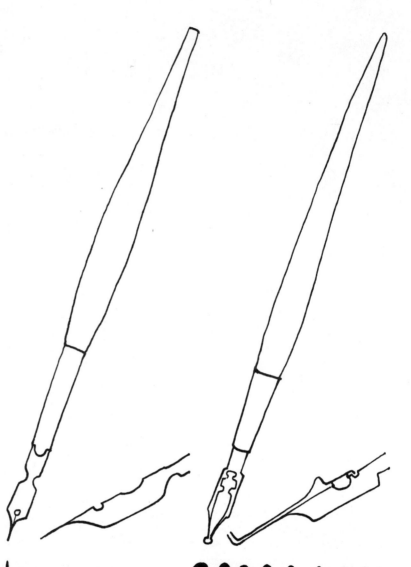

BO B½ B1 B2 B3 B4 B5 B5½ B6

esides LETTERING with a broad-edged pen the letters in Chapters II & III, you will find yourself DRAWING many of the others. Two kinds of points are useful: the pressure-sensitive, variable-width pen; and the fixed-width pen. Crowquills, mapping pens, and pointed brushes need filling or dipping. Technical fountain pens make lines of uniform size with special hollow tubular points.

Gillott makes a selection of pointed flexible drawing nibs for its reservoir pen holder. Pentalic, 132 W. 22nd St, New York, N.Y. 10011. US. distributor.

Speedball offers both a flexible nib and a fixed-width nib in many different sizes. Hunt Mfg Co., 1405 Locust St., Philadelphia, Pa. 19102

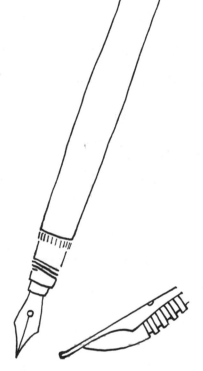

4x0 3x0 00 0 1 2 2½ 3 4 6 7 8 9

The flexible-point Artpen combines the convenience of a fountain pen with the India ink capacity of a dip pen. Koh-I-Noor, 100 North St. Bloomsbury, N.J. 08804

Rapidograph, Mars, Castell TG, & Leroy all offer variations of the technical pen system. Buy only one or two, to keep them unclogged.

The traditional fine-pointed dip pen, if used with care, will make the finest line with the most flexibility. Many styles & brands available.

Choose your ink from one of three categories, depending on the kind of pen you are using.

WATER-SOLUBLE OR FOUNT INDIA:	PERMANENT OR CARBON-BASED:	TECHNICAL AND SPECIAL INDIA:
Schaeffer cartridge	quill	Graphos
Parker cartridge	Braun quill	Art pen
Braun fount quill	Mitchell roundhand,	Rapidograph
Osmiroid	Witch, & scroll	
Platignum	Brause	
Pelikan	Speedball	
	metal crowquill	

Some fiber-tipped markers can be re-inked with spirit-based or water-based inks when their supply dries out.

MAIL ORDER SOURCES:

Pentalic, 132 West 22nd Street, New York, N.Y. 10011

Calligrafree, Box 96, Brookville, Ohio, 45309

REVIEWING the SMALL LETTERS

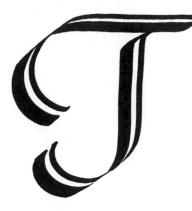 o understand capitals you must always see them in context with small letters. While to a certain extent you can combine any decorative initial with any text letter and make it work visually, for the more ordinary uses — capitalizing sentences and proper nouns — you must employ the proper capital in the proper size. These forms and proportions have been established by custom in your readers' expectations; if you deviate too far from them you will not necessarily be wrong but you may unintentionally be awkward. Don't draw the reader's attention to something in your design unless you MEAN TO.

The alphabets on the following pages have been set up for easy learning, simplified practice, or quick review, depending on your level of expertise. Practice them in the groups suggested here, using a pen nib of this width: ▌ (SEE CHOOSING A PEN). Begin by using the guidelines shown with each alphabet; either fasten a sheet of lightweight paper over the page so that the lines show faintly through, or run multiple copies of

Copy — don't trace.
Practice letters in the groups suggested. Look for family resemblances as well as distinctive characteristics.

guidelines on a duplicator, Xerox, or mimeo machine. To do this, you can rule off your own guidelines by laying the edge of the page over a sheet of paper, penciling two rows of marks, and connecting the marks with a straightedge.

These alphabets & guidelines have been proportioned to fit the capitals in Chapter III. Do not try to practice without guidelines or with different guidelines until you are thoroughly familiar with the basics of each alphabet. When you begin to try paper of different sizes, quotations of different lengths, & pens of different

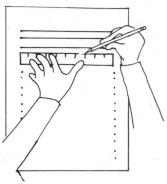

Ruling a sheet for practice paper guidelines.

widths, you can rescale the letters to fit any pen you already have, and draw new guidelines. Just follow the pen-width markings at the beginning of every alphabet, using the pen you want. Master these alphabets— or at least make sure you understand them thoroughly—before attempting the capitals of Chapter III. Notice their differences and similarities; observe how they are spaced; pay attention to the relative style of the capital and the small letter.

Scaling for different pen sizes

abcdefg

abcd

ab

Pen angle
20°

Ascenders and descenders extend only slightly
beyond letter body.

Wedge-shaped Celtic serif
is made of two over-
lapping strokes.

abcdefghíj

celtic capitals
appear on
page 31.

these marks to
portion new guide
for any size nib.

If you are nimble, turn pen angle gradually throughout stroke   to   flatten end.

klmnopqr

Runic
capitals
appear
on page 33.

stuvwxyz

PRACTICE GROUPS: o1 abcdegpq hmnruwy fijkt svxz

Use these marks to
rule off guide'lines
for practice paper
with 2mm (⅛") nib.

Pen angle

45°

Double Gothic capitals appear on page 35.

abcdefghijklmno

White space inside and between letters is as wide as black stroke of letter itself.

Compound Capitals appear on page 37.

pqrstuvwxyz

PRACTICE GROUPS:

obdgpq sz
acer hkmn
fijtzl uvwy

Strokes only touch at corners, not overlap.

Pen angle 45°

abcdefghijklmno

White space inside and between letters is as wide as black stroke of letter itself.

Double Gothic capitals appear on page 35.

pqrstuvwxyz

PRACTICE GROUPS:

obdgpq   sz
acer   hkmn
fijtxl   uvwy

Compound capitals appear on page 37.

Strokes only touch at corners, not overlap.

Pen angle 45°

Italic swash capitals appear on page 41

abcdefghijklm

Swashes are optional on bfhkl

nopqrstuvwxyz

PRACTICE GROUPS: acdegquy bhkmnpr fijlt osvwxz

Pen angle /45°

abcdefghijklmnopqr

Italic
Scroll
capitals
appear
on page 39.

stuvwxyz

PRACTICE GROUPS: acdegquy fijlt
bhkmnpr osvwxz

Pen angle

Roman capitals appear on page 29

Retouched Roman capitals appear on page 43.

Constructed Roman capitals appear on page 49.

45°

Keep serif at end of straight strokes, light enough not to overpower letter.

abcdefghijklmn

'm' is a little narrower than 2 'n's would be.

opqrstuvwxyz

PRACTICE GROUPS: oce ilbdpq atfrhmnuj
sg vwxyzk

Pen angle 45°

abcdefghijklmn

Squared Bookhand capitals appear on page 47.

opqrstuvwxyz

PRACTICE GROUPS: oce bdpqil atfrhnmujy szgxk uw

Pen angle /40°

Ronde capitals appear on page 51.

abcdefghijklm

nopqrstuvwxyz

PRACTICE GROUPS: ocexad mnuit   vw
&fhjklpqy rsz

Pen angle
45°

serifs are made of two strokes

abcdefghijklmnopqrstuvwxyz

Legende
capitals
appear
on page 33.

PRACTICE GROUPS:
adhkmnsu vwx   rtz yg
ocbeq   fjtli

Copyright Margaret Shepherd

Bibliography

Degering, Hermann, Lettering. New York: Pentalic, 1965.

Douglass, Ralph, Calligraphic Lettering. New York: Watson-Guptill, 1949.

Drogin, Marc, Medieval Calligraphy. New Jersey: Schram, 1980.

Gourdie, Tom, Calligraphic Styles. New York: Pentalic, 1979.

Ismar, David, Our Calligraphic Heritage. New York: Geyer Studio, 1979.

Munch, Gary, Hand-to-Hand Combat. Eugene, Oregon: Instant Incunable, 1980.

Friedrich, Neugebauer, The Mystic Art of Written Forms. Boston: Neugebauer, 1980

Shepherd, Margaret, Learning Calligraphy. New York: Macmillan, 1978.

Studley, Vance, Left-handed Calligraphy. New York: Van Nostrand Reinhold, 1979.

Wong, Frederick, The Complete Calligrapher. New York: Watson-Guptill, 1980.

2500 YEARS of PEN CAPITALS

en-lettered capitals have changed abundantly over the centuries after the first inklings of a distinction between a majuscule and a minuscule began to appear. The characteristics of the broad-edge pen have not prevented the alphabet from manifesting itself in at least a dozen different basic capital styles and hundreds of variations. Some, like Greek, Roman, and Italic, can be used without small letters and still retain their legibility; others, like Gothic Doubled Stroke and Compound Initials, assume star quality and appear to advantage if used sparingly; a few, like Ronde, function best only when used with their matching small letters & look incongruous with any others.

The capitals on the following 26 pages have been designed for practice with a wide pen (▌), a narrow pen (Ι), a scroll pen (ΙΙ), and a pointed or non-variable-width pen in narrow or medium width (Ι). For all but the Scroll letters, use the guidelines provided on the capitals page and on the suggested matching page of small letters, either by fastening a sheet of lightweight paper over the page so that the guidelines below show faintly through, or by making multiple copies on a mimeo, Xerox, or duplicator machine. (Pencil your guideline sheets first by using the marks at the edge of the page as a pattern.)

PRE-ROMAN GREEK AND ETRUSCAN STRUCTURE.

Fifth century, B.C., kylix painting of scholar.

Third century, B.C., papyrus letters.

TO UNDERSTAND CAPITALS, STUDY THEIR ANCESTORS. PEN CALLIGRAPHY DERIVES ITS FORMS AND ITS VERY NAME FROM THE GREEK WORDS FOR "BEAUTIFUL" (KALI) AND "WRITING" OR "INSCRIPTION" (GRAPHOS), WITH EMPHASIS AT FIRST ON THE CARVED QUALITY OF THE LETTERS. THEY LACK A CLEAR VERTICAL ORIENTATION, OFTEN APPEARING ON A SLANT, UPSIDE-DOWN, OR BACK-WARDS; STROKES HAVE NO VARIATION BETWEEN THICK AND THIN; LETTER FORMS SHOW ONLY A HINT OF THE SQUARE ARCHITECTURAL CONSTRUCTION OF CLASSIC ROMAN CAPITALS; LETTERS FREQUENTLY IGNORE ANY STRICT HORIZONTAL GUIDELINES; BUT STILL MOST OF THE ALPHABET WE KNOW TODAY IS PRESENT IN EM-BRYONIC FORM. WITH HALF A DOZEN MODERNIZED ADDITIONS, IT IS WRITE-ABLE AND READABLE TODAY. FAMILIARITY WITH IT GIVES BOTH WRITER AND READER A QUICK REFRESHER COURSE IN SOME OF THE ORIGINS OF THE CLASSIC ROMAN CAPITAL.

The bold-face alphabet is Roman; the light-face alphabet is a composite of old, new, & invented Greek.

ROMAN LETTERFITTING

ADVENT
Twentieth century, trademark.

First century, carved letters from a tomb of a legionary.

LONG BEFORE THE EMERGENCE OF REAL INITIAL CAPITALS, ROMAN LETTERS — BOTH CARVED & WRITTEN — SHOWED THE ABILITY TO ALTER THEIR SIZE AND PLACEMENT TO SUIT VISUAL DEMANDS. BECAUSE FORMAL CAPITALS HAVE NO LEEWAY FOR NARROWING OR WIDENING THE LETTERS TO MAKE LINES COME OUT THE DESIRED LENGTH, LINE LENGTH IS CONTROLLED BY MANIPULATING THE SPACE AROUND THE LETTERS. LETTERS CAN BE JOINED IN PAIRS, REDUCED & RAISED OR LOWERED, ENLARGED BY LENGTHENING OR HEIGHTENING ONE STROKE, AND COMPRESSED TO FIT INTO OTHER LETTERS. GRACEFUL SPACING CAN BE QUIETLY EMPHASIZED — AND AWKWARD LETTER COMBINATIONS RESHAPED. THE FORMAL ROMANS ACQUIRE NEW APPEAL THROUGH THIS RELAXED AND SPONTANEOUS TREATMENT OF THE SPACES BETWEEN LETTERS.

PRACTICE GROUPS: ILEF ODBP CG HT KQR JU S MNAVWXYZ

SOME PRACTICE GROUPS FOR LETTERFITTING: II IO OO LT LA RV RA QU

Small letters: page 20.

CELTIC COMMONCASE

quam fructum esse manduca, et
diebant discipuli eius :·
venunt in jerusolimam
et cum introise templum

variant forms of D, N, and M in the eighth-century Book of Kells

CELTIC LETTERS OCCUPY A KIND OF NO-MAN'S-
LAND BETWEEN CAPITAL AND SMALL LETTERS.
MANY APPEAR ON THE SAME PAGE IN TWO
OR EVEN THREE DIFFERENT FORMS — OFTEN
ACCORDING TO THEIR POSITION & FUNCTION,
SOMETIMES NOT. ENLARGED INITIALS ALSO
ARE DRAWN FROM THE FULL RANGE OF VAR-
IANTS AVAILABLE. (MODERN TYPOGRAPHERS
HAVE REDISCOVERED THIS APPROACH WITH
THE INNOVATIVE 'COMMONCASE' LAYOUT,
WHERE ALL LETTERS ARE THE SAME HEIGHT.)
WITH CELTIC, TWO DISTINCT SETS OF LETTERS
ARE SLOWLY EMERGING; BUT THEY ARE STILL
USED IN THE TEXT ALMOST INTERCHANGEABLY
THE DEFINITION OF A "CAPITAL" LETTER THUS
DEPENDS MORE ON ITS COLOR, SIZE, WEIGHT,
PLACEMENT, AND DECORATION, THAN ON A
SEPARATE SET OF SPECIALIZED LETTERFORMS.

Small letters: page 15.

CELTIC RUNES

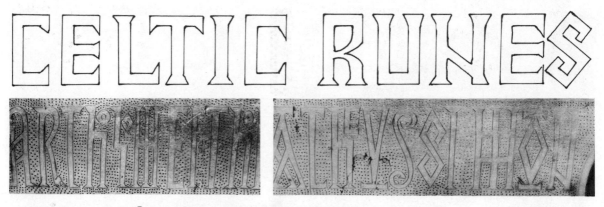

Runes from rim of Ardagh chalice, eighth century

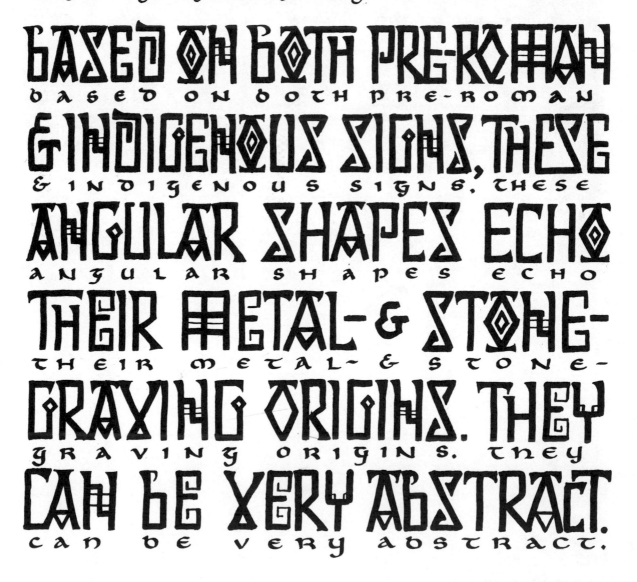

BASED ON BOTH PRE-ROMAN
based on both pre-roman

& INDIGENOUS SIGNS, THESE
& indigenous signs, these

ANGULAR SHAPES ECHO
angular shapes echo

THEIR METAL- & STONE-
their metal- & stone-

GRAVING ORIGINS. THEY
graving origins. they

CAN BE VERY ABSTRACT.
can be very abstract.

Note how runic forms echo the angular graven Greek letters.

Draw with a pointed pen, or turn a wide pen at flat and right angles.

Small letters: page 15.

Gothic Doubled Stroke

Fifteenth century, Juan de Yciar Sixteenth century, Giovanni Battista Palatino Sixteenth century

Gothic Capitals, whether Buried in the Text or Enlarged as Decorated Initials, are given Extra Emphasis by Doubling the Main Stroke in Exact Parallel. Further Ornament is applied with the Pen Turned Sideways or a Smaller Point, and always Echoes the Heavy Texture of the Gothic Black Letter Page.

ABCDEFG

To achieve accurate doubling, watch white, not black, areas take shape.

HIJKLMN

Note resemblance to Celtic shapes.

OPQRSTU

VWXYZ

PRACTICE GROUPS: OCEGQT HUNY AVXSZ BDRP FIJKL MW

Copyright Margaret Shepherd

Small letters: pages 16 and 17.

COMPOUND INITIALS

From a fifteenth-century German Bible

These initials, in contrast to the Doubled strokes of the previous page, represent an important step in the direction of a DRAWN rather than a WRITTEN capital. Not only the letter but the stroke itself holds an outlined white space for ink, paint, ornament, or gold to illuminate the form of the letter.

Note how letters tend to conform to circular outlines.

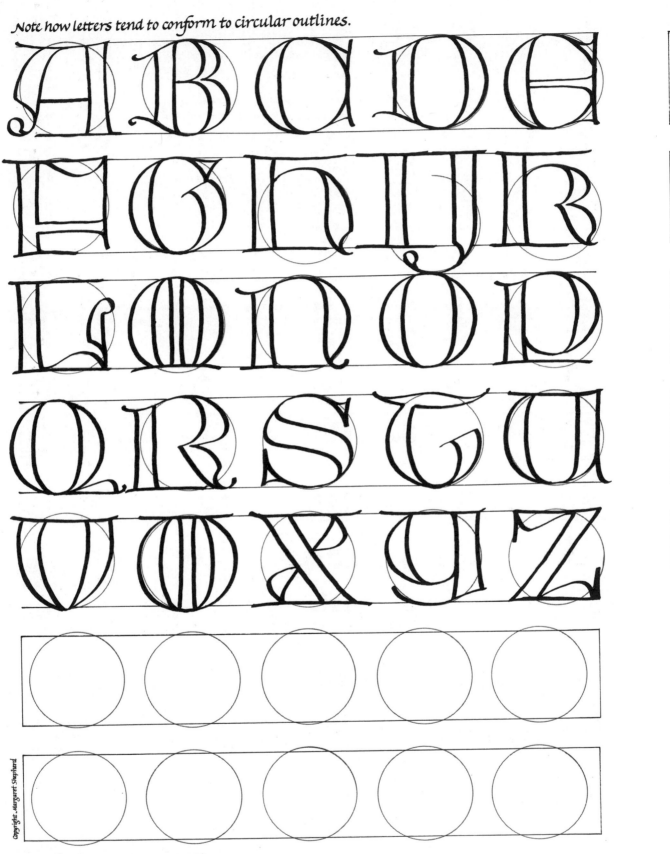

Small letters: pages 16 and 17.

ITALIC SCROLLWRITING

Twentieth century, document heading
Author's design.

WHEREAS:

The double-pointed "SCROLL PEN" can teach you new things about the familiar ITALIC CAPITALS. Watch carefully how clearly it shows your pen angle and how precise your stroke joins have to be. Avoid overlapping strokes, open-ended strokes, compound strokes, and constricted curves.

Leave diagonal junctions open.　　　　Close up vertical strokes with short sideways motion.

First five rows are enlarged to show construction of letters in last two rows.

Small letters: page 19.

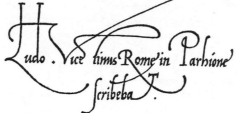

Sixteenth century, swash capitals by Ludovico degli Arrighi.

Swash capitals fall into two categories — those whose swashes are added to a simple Italic capital, and those whose swashes alter the letter's basic shape. The best way to use swash capitals is to let them perform solo; if you must write a word or a whole line of them, do not swash every letter. To preserve the calligraphic style of the letter, pay attention to joins so that each swash shows the transition from thick to thin. With repetitive swashes, strive for accurate parallel lines — and then break up this rhythm with an occasional odd stroke.

3° slant

A B C D E F

Keep joins thin, not overlapping, to accentuate the undulating line of the swash.

G H I J K L M

Some letters' swashes are interchangeable.

N O P Q R S T

U V W X Y Z

PRACTICE GROUPS: BDRP CGE AHM TIJ UVWFK OQ XVYN SLZ

Small letters: page 18.

RETOUCHED ROMAN

Nineteenth century, carved Roman letter

Fifteenth century, Roman letter printed from woodblock

Twentieth century, retouched Roman letter

Scribes of the Italian Renaissance, in search of a capital to accompany their humanistic Bookhand, drew inspiration from classical Roman inscriptions. Originally carved in stone from wide brush-lettered outlines, Roman capitals were carefully translated into ink & paper with broad pen & crowquill.

Use these marks to proportion new guide lines for any size nib.

Copyright Margaret Shepherd

Small letters: page 20.

ENGLISH TWO-PLY
ICELANDIC TWO-PLY

KING HARALD
and the
ICELANDERS

Translated from the Icelandic
by Pardee Lowe, Jr. with original wood engravings by
Michael McCurdy

Penmaen Press, Limited

EAST TO
AMERICA

*Twentieth century,
author's design*　　　*Twentieth century, book
title design by Ed Smith*

Here are two designs that represent just the tip of a calligraphic iceberg, the 'Roman' capital made of two pen strokes. As shown here, this 'two-ply' alphabet carries on existing traditions from Gothic: first, the doubled parallel strokes that leave a thin stripe of white in between them; second, the symmetrically curving pair of strokes that meet and overlap along the center. Either way, the names 'ENGLISH' and 'ICELANDIC' are invented to represent these two related design effects — one controlled and refined, the other rougher, stronger, and more primitive. Further variations on the two-stroke Roman can evoke other 'nationalities.' The accompanying Bookhand text letter can be constructed of two strokes to match the style of the capital or just given a heavy serif to add weight to it.

English two-ply is lighter and more refined, like English wool.

Icelandic two-ply has the dense, bulky character of Icelandic wool.
Both alphabets are twentieth-century designs that evoke the seventeenth & eighteenth centuries.

Copyright. Margaret Shepherd

Small letters: page 20.

Squared Bookhand

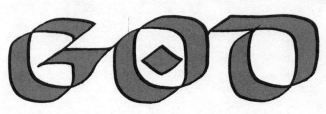

Twentieth century, author's design

Twentieth century, book cover

Bell Publishing Co.

With the advent of typography &
printing, Bookhand, in the form of
'lowercase Roman', became accept-
ed as the standard letters of post-
Renaissance Europe. They appear,
however, in a multitude of letter
bodies, including this squared-off
shape. The matching capitals evoke
the classic forms of Roman, the com-
pactness of Celtic, and the angular-
ity and rigid conformity of Gothic.
Keep the corners squarely rounded and make the thin joins precise.

ABCDEFGHIJ

Keep joins sharp and thin.

KLMNOPQRS

TUUWXYZ

Small letters: page 21.

Constructed Roman Capitals for Bookhand

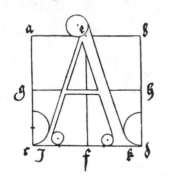

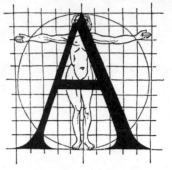

Sixteenth century, Albrecht Dürer   Sixteenth century, Geofroy Tory, Champ Fleury

For 500 years since the invention of type and the printing press, calligraphers and designers have striven to harmonize the Roman capitals with the Bookhand lowercase letters. While a pen-lettered capital works well within blocks of text, sometimes a capital must be drawn for use as a headline or a display initial. A classic or 'old style' capital is drawn to approximate the curves and proportions imposed by a pen; a constructed or 'modern' capital derives its shape from geometric measurements. Be cautious in combining them; one instrument-drawn line begets another until sooner or later the touch of the human hand and broad-edged pen is eradicated. Constructed capitals ought to enhance calligraphy, not imitate typography.

Classic Modern

Small letters: page 20.

French Ronde

A B C D E F G H I J K L M
N O P Q R S T U V X Y Z

Nineteenth century, "Escritura Redonda"

A popular script and type style
after 1700, Ronde shows the in~
fluence of both the calligraphy pen
and the engraver's tool. Each capital is fiercely individualistic,
setting its own construction rules.
Used with care & restraint, this
style has an old~world charm,
but easily becomes too Rococo. ~

Do not make letters any heavier than shown here.

Make round endings with corner of pen while ink is wet, or use smaller pen.

Small letters: page 22.

Legende Freehand

Peter Matthiessen
The Snow Leopard

Twentieth century, book title

This style not only bridges the traditional gap between handwriting and formal calli- graphy, it opens two-way traffic on the road between type and lettering. Calligraphy can borrow from many type designs, adapting them freely to give new challenge and new shape to the determining rules of the pen. This hybrid alphabet harmonizes the two- stroke serif, the Gothic compact letterbody, the Italic slant, and the Islamic swash?

Note how strokes overlap

Small letters: page 23

Bibliography

Baker, Arthur, Historic Calligraphic Alphabets. New York: Dover, 1980.

Cresci, Giovan Francesco, A Renaissance Alphabet. With an introduction by Donald M. Anderson. Madison: University of Wisconsin Press, 1971.

Dürer, Albrecht, On the Just Shaping of Letters. New York: Dover, 1965.

Macdonald, Byron J., Calligraphy: The Art of Lettering with the Broad Pen. New York: Pentalic, 1978

Nesbitt, Alexander, The History and Technique of Lettering. New York: Dover, 1950.

Ogg, Oscar, Three Classics of Italian Calligraphy. New York: Dover, 1953.

Svaren, Jacqueline, Written Letters: 22 Alphabets for Calligraphers. Freeport, Maine: Bond-Wheelwright, 1975.

DRAWING a DECORATED INITIAL

ith the drawn capital, the scribe no longer relies on the solid stroke of the broad-edge calligraphy pen to determine the shape, color, and texture of the letter. While most drawn capitals grow from the forms of their pen-lettered models, many bear only a distant resemblance to their calligraphic ancestors, often mirroring much more clearly the decorative arts of their own generation.

The categories of letters on the following pages build on techniques already outlined in Chapter III for Compound Initials, Constructed Capitals, Retouched Roman, and Scrollwriting. With a number of approaches, scribes begin to sharpen and refine the fundamental pen letter. Minor inaccuracies and awkward joins unremarkable in a text-sized capital become glaring distractions in an enlarged initial, and carefully-drawn ornament demands an equally finished quality in the letter that it decorates.

At right: compound, constructed, retouched, & scroll capitals

Basic pen letter

egin with the Roman pen form of the letter as a foundation. Draw an outline around it. This is the point of departure for many decorated initials. The outline can be manipulated in many different ways. First, the letter itself can be made narrower or wider in its basic proportions. Second, the width & shape of the stroke can be altered. Third, the weight of the outlining pen can make the letter look different. And finally, small variations in the drawing of the serifs can have a pro-

Narrower or wider letter width

Heavier or lighter stroke width

Heavier br lighter outline weight

Variation of serif shape

nounced effect on the character of the whole letter. Serifs can be extended to close up open letters or letter spaces.

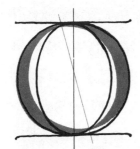

ne of the most common modifications made to the Roman pen capital is rotation of the natural axis of symmetry. Most pen capitals are written with a pen angle between 15° and 50°. Drawn capitals flatten this.

Other letters show the effect of making them symmetrical along a vertical axis. A center line in pencil helps keep the letter well-balanced.

Symmetrical letter construction

eanwhile, a few adjustments help reconcile some asymmetrical letters to the general style, by reinterpreting structural lines from the original letter as decorative lines in the drawn version. Note extended serifs.

Stylization of legs and tails

Roman letter shapes lie behind many drawn capitals.

lthough Roman letters are the source for many drawn initials, Celtic capitals exert strong influence on basic forms. While early drawn capitals follow the original pen-lettered prototypes in outline and in asymmetry, later versions are balanced and formal. But the closed, rounded nature of the letter persists; if we see the Roman capital as a STRUCTURE, then the Celtic is a CONTAINER.

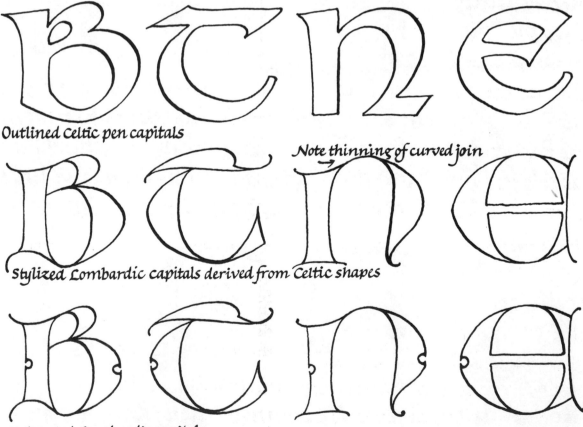

Outlined Celtic pen capitals

Note thinning of curved join

Stylized Lombardic capitals derived from Celtic shapes

Elaborated Lombardic capitals

o matter what the basic form of the drawn capital, it defines three important kinds of two-dimensional space: inside the letter body, inside the letter stroke, and outside the letter body.

Space inside the letter body can be filled with repeating or random allover texture, or abstract stylized decoration. Space within the letter stroke can be similarly ornamented or double-outlined. Space outside the letter can be freely embellished or boxed off in a variety of containing shapes,

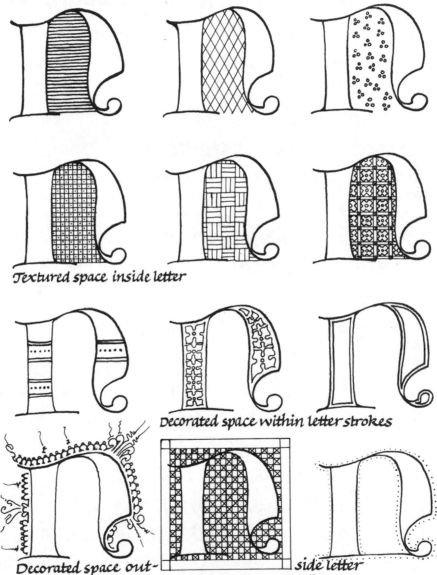

Textured space inside letter

Decorated space within letter strokes

Decorated space out-
side letter

which can match what fills the space inside the letter body, or contrast with it.

nother kind of space exists around a drawn letter—the third dimension. In an important conceptual transformation, the early medieval page stops being flat and starts acquiring depth. The letter lies on page level but it may contain flat overlapping, knotted, braided, or interwoven elements. It can contain scenes that seem to extend far behind the page, through naturalistic portrayal of a landscape or a building, a contrasting use of large figures up close & small figures far away, or representation of converging lines of perspective. An intermediate kind of three-dimensional letter presents real material, such as foliage, flowers, & small objects, raised in shallow relief—as a rule of thumb, the more life-like & less abstract a rendering is, the more it will appear raised from the surface of the page. A Roman

3-dimensional figure   Perspective

Flat raised foliage   Rounded raised foliage

Incised letter   Floating letter

capital, in contrast, makes use of light and shadow to give an imitation carved effect. Finally, the letter itself can appear to be floating somewhere slightly in front of the page if it is given a trompe l'oeil shadow below.

esign ideas for flat pattern, texture, and shallow relief are all around the scribe or miniaturist, in the everyday visual environment. They can be adapted from almost any source: textiles, architectural ornament, and home furnishings. Sensitize your eye to what you can absorb from surface pattern around you. Watch for how pattern elements repeat, contrast, orient

to the vertical, and fit each other. Notice also how flat pattern relates to other flat or three-dimensional elements that may appear to lie in front or in back of the pattern surface. If you can pay attention objectively to the psychological processes by which your eye interprets pattern and depth in nature, you can be both forceful and precise when you put pattern and depth into the spaces of your capital letter designs.

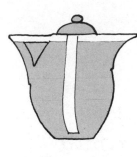he decorated initial modulates imperceptibly from letter into picture. Many realistic elements can be used to ornament the structure of the letter stroke: vines, trees, flowers, birds, fish, beasts real or mythical, architectural detail, cords, jewels, banners, household objects, and human beings classical or contemporary.

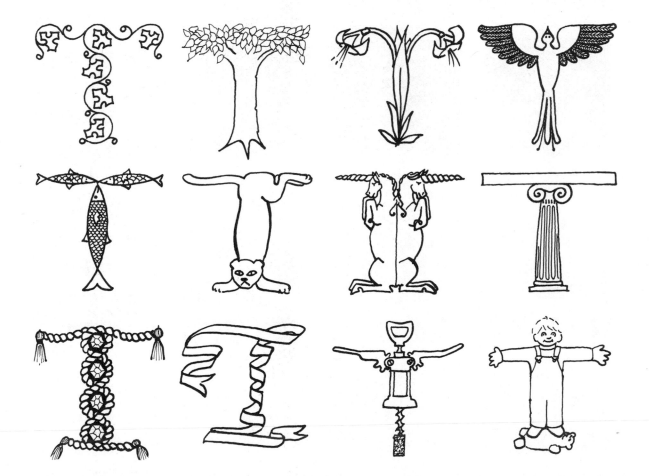

With each kind of realistic letter, the scribe can manipulate the viewer's reaction, balancing recognition of an object against comprehension of the letter it represents.

o not let a preoccupation with the rich tradition of the illuminated capital keep you from appreciating the purely visual qualities of the letters themselves. Letters often make beautiful abstract shapes ; sometimes familiar objects unexpectedly make letters. Keep your eye and your mind — and your sense of humor — warmed up to appreciate the hidden letter

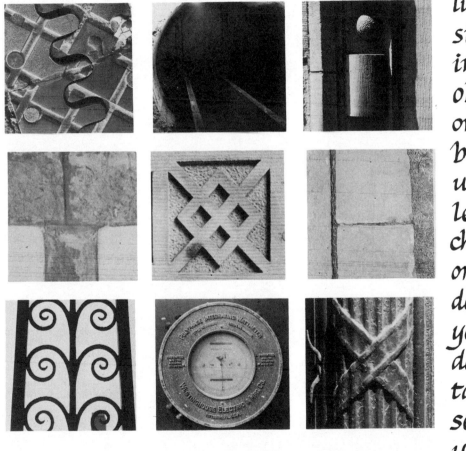 lurking inside every inanimate object. Not only will you build up a unique collection of charming & original letter designs, but you will also develop a talent for seeing beyond mere

superficial identification of things in the world around you. Instead, you can be exercising the talent for SEEING the shape & visual potential of every form.

Bibliography

Gray, Nicolete, Lettering as Drawing. Contour
          and Silhouette and The Moving
          Line. New York: Oxford, 1970.
Jackson, Donald, The Story of writing. New York:
          Taplinger, 1981.
Johnston, Edward, Writing and Illuminating
          and Lettering. New York: Pentalic, 1976.
Lamb, C. M., The Calligrapher's Handbook.
          London: Faber, 1968.

PLACING CAPITALS on the PAGE

Capitals—even the most individualistic—still must harmonize with each other and with the small letters they accompany. Furthermore, whether pen-lettered or drawn-and-filled-in, they must harmonize with the layout of the page. The most carefully drawn and elaborately ornamented initial can still strike a sour note if it is placed wrong on the page. All the forms presented so far remain to be pulled together with a fluent and graceful page layout.

How can the scribe develop expertise in integrating capitals into the whole page? The answer is two-fold: through learning to think and to sketch. First, think about all the elements a quotation presents to you as the idea for the page takes shape: the mood of the passage, the historical era of the author or the topic, the shape of the initial, the length of the text. One of these will suggest a starting point. Second, sketch the resulting idea, very roughly, with a little 'thumbnail sketch.' The two illustrations at right show sketches for designs on pages 69 & 72.

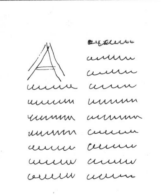

A PAGE LETTERED ONLY IN
CAPITALS HAS A CERTAIN
QUALITY OF RESERVE; IT
IS RESTFUL TO THE EYE OF
THE BEHOLDER, THOUGH
NOT NECESSARILY TO THE
HAND OF THE CALLIGRAPH-
ER! THE LETTERS MAKE A
SOFT, EVEN TEXTURE ON
THE PAGE, A VERY SUBTLE
EFFECT. BUT PROPORTION
OF BOTH TEXT AREA AND
INDIVIDUAL LETTERS MUST
BE NEARLY FLAWLESS....

QUITE A DIFFERENT EFFECT IS ACHIEVED WHEN EVEN JUST ONE LETTER IS EMPHA-SIZED. LIKE SPICE IN A STEW, IT NOT ONLY ADDS A TASTE OF ITS OWN BUT ALSO ALTERS THE FLAVOR OF THE OTHER INGREDI-ENTS. ENLARGING THE 'Q' ABOVE CHANGES THE BALANCE AND IMPACT OF THE ENTIRE PAGE....

ith the emergence of a true capital we find letters that have fourfold emphasis to distinguish them from text letters: they are large in size, they are different in form, they are decorated with ornament, & they are accented with color. They do for the page what jewels do for a cloak....

As the capital letters (majuscules) get larger, the small ones (minuscules) get smaller. By now there are 2 distinct forms for many letters.

A few medium-size (but clearly capital) letters bridge the visual gap. Carolingian ornamentation begins to be less governed by the shape of the capital letter and more related to the shape of its background....

begin to dominate the page, crowding out the letters with elaborate and exquisite miniature painting....

With the invention of moveable type, Capitals become a separate element on the page—both visually and technically.

Ⅴisually, the typesetter is duty-bound to put them in just where they occur, cannot stretch or squeeze a line in the scribe's natural manner. The layout of the page is somewhat outside the typesetter's control by now.

Ⅴechnically, capitals straddle the divide between the handlettered book & the printed book in a number of ways. Using a small letter as a cue, a skilled illuminator can then fill the space with a hand-painted decorated capital.

Or, more likely, the capital can be pen-lettered with a few strokes.

Another kind of approach, a woodcut capital, harmonizes with the heavy texture of the smaller text letters. A woodcut in two colors is delicate enough to provide contrast with the text letters, and let light into the page. The design of a two-column traditional page, with the capitals dotted about on the left margins, can be mastered by a calligrapher with a repertoire of strong, square, decorative but unspectacular and interchangeable initials.

 ITH BOOKHAND, WE SEE A CLEAR, THREE-LEVELED stratification of capital design & use. First, the lower case Roman style has its own capitals for use in the text area. Second, larger Roman capitals are used in headings without any smaller letters. Third, a decorated (but not so decorated as formerly) initial dominates the page. The overall effect is light, yet rich and varied to the eye...

The scribe that hones his knife to cut a quill,

And rules his parchment, grinds his ink by hand,

To copy out a sonnet — do what he will,

Cannot escape the preordained demand

To place the capitals exactly where

The poet put them first. He dare not change

A letter or a line. His only care

Lies in the decision to arrange

Fourteen initial letters or just one.

Unless the fourteen might line up to spell

Some unexpected word that he should shun,

Starting each line with 'caps' will serve him well.

The scribe can beautify the poem most

If he acts as its guest and not its host...

as initials, a

victorian favorite for embroidery and engraving . . . .

One or two or three capitals can be featured and decorated

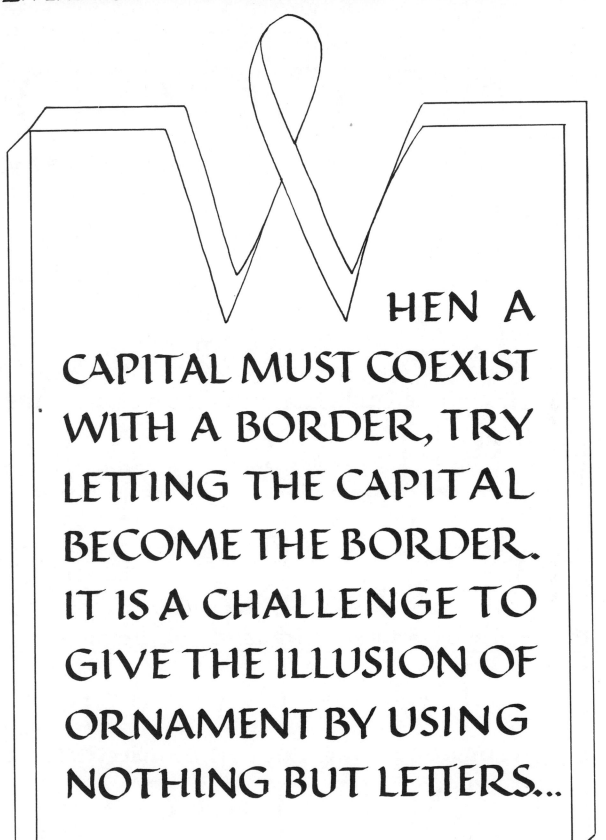

WHEN A CAPITAL MUST COEXIST WITH A BORDER, TRY LETTING THE CAPITAL BECOME THE BORDER. IT IS A CHALLENGE TO GIVE THE ILLUSION OF ORNAMENT BY USING NOTHING BUT LETTERS...

ONE GOOD

It balances them visually, provides a striking but very

WAY TO LAY

readable texture, suits many texts, and springs from

OUT TWO

a long established calligraphic tradition of scribbling

UNEQUAL

between the lines; scholars (and others) annotate

PARAGRAPHS

their source books with translations, commentary,

IS TO INTER-

disagreements, jottings, and other marginalia...

LEAVE THEM.

A
page
can have
a capital in
it without
really con-
taining it!
There are

Take   other ways
advantage   to convey
of   information
the   to the eye
fact   than by an
that   ink-drawn
the   outline. An
eye   outline is
is   just a kind
accustomed   of code for
to   the shape of
stopping   a mass. Why
at   not present
a   the mass it-
straight   self and let
left- Then add the cross-stroke.   the eye do
hand   the work of
margin   perceiving
for an outline.   where that outline lies?...

CAPITALS DON'T HAVE TO BE STRAIGHT-JACKETED INTO ARBITRARY SIZE CATEGORIES. THEY CAN BE INTER-MIXED & FREELY MANIPULATED...

IMAGINATION
is more important
than knowledge.

Albert Einstein

You're in the 20th century. Why write medieval capitals? The initial doesn't always have to come at the beginning...

Bibliography

Baltimore Museum, Two Thousand Years of
        Calligraphy. New York: Pentalic, 1980.

Child, Heather, Calligraphy Today. New York,
        Pentalic, 1976.

Degering, Hermann, Lettering. New York: Pentalic,
        1965.

Drogin. Marc, Medieval Calligraphy. New Jersey:
        Schram, 1980.

Modern Scribes and Lettering Artists. New
        York: Pentalic, 1980.

Shepherd, Margaret, Borders for Calligraphy.
        New York: Macmillan, 1980.

AN ABECEDARY of CAPITALS

Many capitals are one of a kind; scribes collect and study them not as part of an alphabet but as individual works of art. Each has been invented to fill a particular spot in a specific context without regard for how its structure might harmonize with the forms of other letters. Other capitals fit into a partial alphabet as a set of letters that recur throughout a manuscript or a printed book—sharing some common elements while maintaining their individual idiosyncracies. Finally, some letters have been extracted from complete alphabets.

The letters in this highly subjective collection have been chosen to represent a multitude of styles, sources, & eras. They can be embellished or simplified as shown here, or transformed into other letters. Decorative elements from one letter can be transplanted to another letter. Letters that resemble each other may be traded.

Above: basic letter design
Below: variations

Nineteenth century, English. Drawn from William Moon's raised alphabet for the blind.

Tenth century, French. Drawn from a V in The Art of Illuminating, W. R. Tymms. (Day, 1860)

Eighth century, Italian. Drawn from an H in Lettering as Drawing, Nicolete Gray. (Oxford, 1970)

Fifteenth century, Italian. Drawn from Lettering in Ornament, Lewis Day. (Batsford, 1902)

Twentieth century, American, author's design.

Twelfth century, English. Drawn from anonymous twentieth century plaque.

Twentieth century, American, author's design.

Eighth century, Irish; The Book of Kells, Trinity College, Dublin. Drawn from The Book of Kells. (Knopf, 1974)

Fifteenth century, German; Psalter, Fust and Schöff. Drawn from The Art of Illuminating, W. R. Tym (Day, 1860)

Twentieth century, American, author's design.

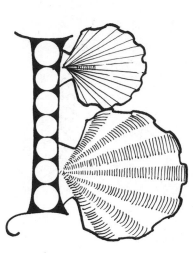

Twentieth century, American, author's design.

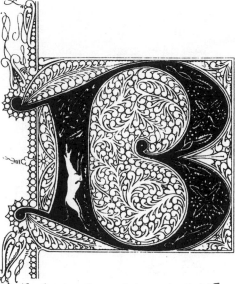

Fifteenth century, German; Psalter, Fust and Schöffer. From Fine Books, Alan G. Thomas. (Weidenfeld, 1967)

Eleventh century, Anglo-Saxon; Psalter, British Museum. Drawn from facsimile.

Fourteenth century, Italian; The Visconti Hours, National Library, Florence. Drawn from The Visconti Hours. (Braziller, 1972)

Eighth century, French; Library of France #626. Drawn from The Art of Illuminating, W. R. Tymms. (Day, 1860)

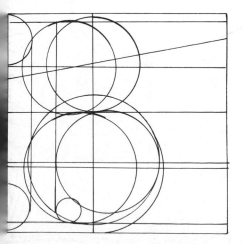

Sixteenth century, German, Johann Neudörffer. Drawn from The Art of Written Forms, Donald Anderson. (Holt, 1969)

Fourteenth century, Italian; The Visconti Hours, National Library, Florence. Drawn from The Visconti Hours. (Braziller, 1972)

Thirteenth century, French? Drawn from Suggestions for Illuminating, W. Randle Harrison. (Vincent, 1907)

Thirteenth century, English. Psalter MS. B. 11.4, f 100, Trinity College Library, Cambridge. Drawn from facsimile.

Sixteenth century, Peruvian; Antonio Ricardo, printer. Drawn from "First Printings of South America in the Harvard Library," Antonio Rodriguez. Harvard Library Bulletin, Volume XVI, #1, January 1968.

Fifteenth century, German. Drawn from The Art of Illuminating, W. R. Tymms. (Day, 1860)

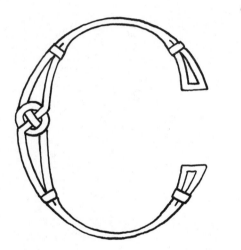

Eighth century, Irish. Drawn from Celtic Art: The Methods of Construction, George Bain. (Dover, 1974)

Fifteenth century, German. Drawn from The Art of Illuminating, W.R. Tymms. (Day, 1860)

Sixteenth century, Italian. Drawn from Three Classics of Italian Calligraphy, Oscar Ogg. (Dover, 1953)

Sixteenth century, French. Drawn from Historic Alphabets & Initials, Carol Belanger Grafton. (Dover, 1977)

Sixteenth century, French. Drawn from an E in Decorative Alphabets and Initials, Alexander Nesbitt. (Dover, 1959)

Eighth century, German. MS. B. 62, Bibliotheca Valli-celliana. Drawn from Lettering as Drawing, Nicolete Gray. (Oxford, 1970)

Twentieth century, German; Jan Tschichold. From Jan Tschichold: Typographer; Rauri McLane. (Godine, 1975)

Fifteenth century, Italian; Mirabilia urbis Romae; Stephan Planck, 1489. Drawn from Five Hundred Years of Printing, S.H.Steinberg. (Penguin, 1977)

Twentieth century, American; Ben Shahn. Drawn from Love and Joy About Letters, Ben Shahn. (Grossman,1965)

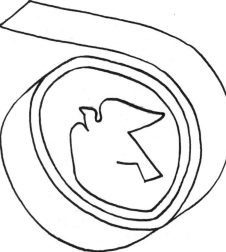

Fifteenth century, French. Drawn from Historic Alphabets & Initials, Carol Belanger Grafton. (Dover, 1977)

Twentieth century, American, author's design.

Fifteenth century, German. The Monastery Press. Drawn from Decorative Initial Letters, A.F. Johnson. (Cresset, 1931)

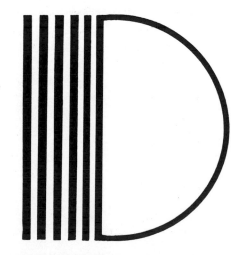

Twentieth century, American, author's design.

Fifteenth century, German. Drawn from Historic Alphabets & Initials, Carol Belanger Grafton. (Dover, 1977)

Twentieth century, American; Paul Renner. Drawn from a sample showcard in the Boston Public Library.

Sixteenth century, Italian. Drawn from an E in The
Historic Alphabets & Initials, Carol Belanger
Grafton. (Dover, 1977)

Fifteenth century, Italian. Metropolitan Museum
of Art, New York. Drawn from facsimile.

Fifteenth century, Italian. Drawn from an E in The
History and Technique of Lettering, Alexander
Nesbitt. (Dover, 1957)

Sixteenth century, French. Drawn from Historic
Alphabets & Initials, Carol Belanger Grafton.
(Dover, 1977)

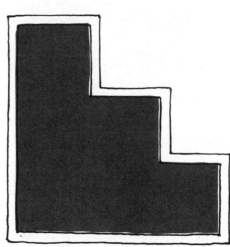

Twentieth century, American. Drawn from a sign
in front of Jericho's Café, New Haven.

FACTVM EST

Twelfth century, Flemish; MS 14790, British Museum.
Drawn from facsimile.

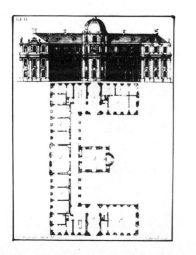

Eighteenth century, German, Johann Steingruber.
From engraved book in the Metropolitan Museum
of Art.

Fifteenth century, Spanish; Juan de Yciar. Drawn from
Decorative Alphabets and Initials, Alexander
Nesbitt. (Dover, 1959)

Sixteenth century, Peruvian; Antonio Ricardo, printer.
Drawn from "First Printings of South America in the
Harvard Library," Antonio Rodriguez. Harvard Library
Bulletin, Volume XVI, #1, January 1968.

Seventeenth century, Portuguese. Drawn from Lettering in Ornament, Lewis Day. (Batsford, 1902)

Tenth century, German. Drawn from Historic Alphabets and Initials, Carol Belanger Grafton. (Dover, 1977)

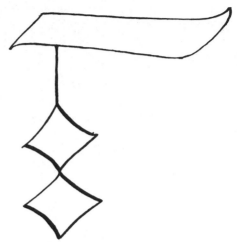

Twentieth century, American, author's design

Sixteenth century, Italian. Drawn from Decorative Alphabets and Initials, Alexander Nesbitt. (Dover, 1959)

Fifteenth century, Italian; Juan de Yciar. Drawn from Historic Alphabets and Initials, Carol Belanger Grafton. (Dover, 1977)

Seventeenth century, English. Drawn from a pew-back in a church in Somersetshire.

Fifteenth century, German. Drawn from The Art of Illuminating, W. R. Tymms. (Day, 1860)

Tenth century, German. Drawn from Two Thousand Years of Calligraphy, Baltimore Museum. (Pentalic, 1980)

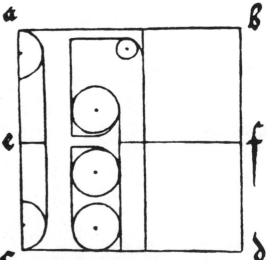

Sixteenth century, German; Albrecht Dürer. From On the Just Shaping of Letters, Albrecht Dürer. (Dover, 1965)

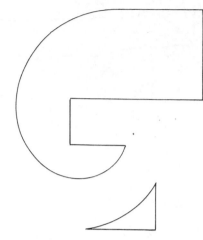

Twentieth century, American, author's design.

Twelfth century, England. Drawn from a tile in Lettering in Ornament, Lewis Day. (Batsford, 1902)

Thirteenth century ? Drawn from an O in a design from Bellerophon Books.

Fifteenth century, English. Add. 15,286, British Museum. Drawn from The Art of Illuminating, W.R. Tymms. (Day, 1860)

Nineteenth century, English; William Morris, The Kelmscott Chaucer. Drawn from Fine Books, Alan G. Thomas. (Weidenfeld, 1967)

Nineteenth century, English; Drawn from an O in Writing and Illuminating and Lettering, Edward Johnston. (Pentalic, 1977)

Eighth century, Continental. Drawn from The Art of Illuminating, W.R. Tymms. (London, 1856)

Fifteenth century, Italian. Drawn from an E in The Visconti Hours. (Braziller, 1972)

Twentieth century, American; Frederic W. Goudy. Drawn from The Alphabet, Frederic W. Goudy. (Dover, 1973)

Thirteenth century? Drawn from an L in a design from Bellerophon Books.

Fifteenth century, Italian; Antonio Cresci. Drawn from Alphabets and Ornaments, Ernst Lehner. (Dover, 1952)

Twentieth century, American. Drawn from a Hennessy Cognac label.

Twentieth century, American, author's design.

Twelfth century, French. Drawn from Medieval Manuscript Painting, Sabrina Mitchell. (Viking, 1964)

Fourteenth century, German. Drawn from The Art of Illuminating, W.R. Tymms. (Day, 1860)

Fourteenth century, French; Missal, Walters Art Gallery. Drawn from Two Thousand Years of Calligraphy, Baltimore Museum. (Pentalic, 1980)

Fifteenth century, Italian; Noctes Atticæ, Aulus Gellius, The Newbury Library. Drawn from Two Thousand Years of Calligraphy, Baltimore Museum. (Pentalic, 1980)

Seventeenth century, Italian; Silvestre; Paris Royal Library. From Florid and Unusual Alphabets. (Dover, 1976)

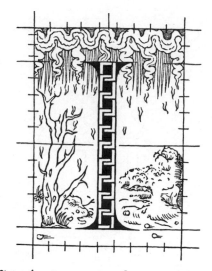

Sixteenth century, French; Geofroy Tory. From Champ Fleury. (Dover, 1967)

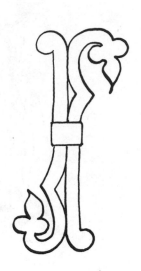

Tenth century, Ottoman; unfinished drawing, ms. Stowe 3. British Museum. Drawn from Lettering as Drawing: Contour and Silhouette, Nicolete Gray. (Oxford, 1970)

Sixteenth century, German. Drawn from Five Hundred Years of Printing, S. H. Steinberg. (Penguin, 1974)

Tenth century, Ottoman; unfinished drawing, ms. Stowe 3, British Museum. Drawn from Lettering as Drawing: Contour and Silhouette, Nicolete Gray. (Oxford, 1970)

Fifteenth century, Italian; Gradual, Kupferstichkabinett, 78.F.1, Dahlem Museum, Berlin. Drawn from The Decorated Letter, J. J. G. Alexander. (Braziller, 1978)

Ninth century, Carolingian; The Metz Gospels, ms. Lat. 9388, Bibliothèque Nationale. Drawn from Lettering as Drawing: Contour and Silhouette, Nicolete Gray. (Oxford, 1970)

Fifteenth century, Italian? Drawn from Lettering in Ornament, Lewis Day. (Batsford, 1902)

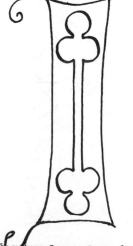

Twelfth century, German. Drawn from The Art of Illuminating, W. R. Tymms. (Day, 1860)

Sixteenth century, German. Anton Neudörffer; Copy Book, Baltimore Museum. Drawn from Two Thousand Years of Calligraphy, Baltimore Museum. (Pentalic, 1980)

Twentieth century, American, author's design.

Twentieth century, American. Drawn from a cyanocitta cristata cristata (Northern Blue Jay) in Field Book of Eastern Birds, L. A. Hausman. (Putnam, 1946)

Twentieth century, American, Larry L. Ogborn. Drawn from a sample showcard in the Boston Public Library.

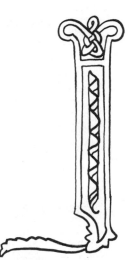

Eleventh century, German; New Testament, Harleian collection # 7,183, British Museum. Drawn from The Art of Illuminating, W.R. Tymms. (Day, 1860)

Sixteenth century, Italian; Amphiario Vespasiano. Drawn from Historic Alphabets & Initials, Carol Belanger Grafton. (Dover, 1977)

Fifteenth century, German;   The Menz Psalter. Drawn from The Art of Illuminating, W.R. Tymms, (Day, 1860)

Fourteenth century, Italian. Drawn from Lettering in Ornament, Lewis Day. (Batsford, 1902)

Fourteenth century, Italian; South Kensington Museum. Drawn from The Art of Illuminating, W.R. Tymms. (Day, 1860)

Sixteenth century, English; A Book Containing Divers Sortes of Handes, John de Beauchesne and John Baildon. Drawn from The Art of Written Forms, Donald M. Anderson. (Holt, 1968)

Nineteenth century, French; Animal Alphabet. Silvestre. From Florid and Unusual Alphabets. (Dover, 1974)

Fifteenth century, Italian. Drawn from Alphabets and Initials, Ernst Lehner. (Dover, 1952)

Fourteenth century, French. Drawn from Alpha and Ornaments, Ernst Lehner. (Dover, 1952)

Fourteenth century, German; Psalter #26, Pierpont Morgan Library. Drawn from catalog.

Eighteenth century, French; Jean Michel Papillon. From Decorative Alphabets and Initials. Alexander Nesbitt. (Dover, 1959)

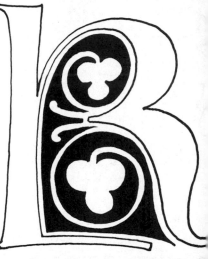

Ninth century, French. Drawn from The Art of Illuminating, W. R. Tymms. (Day, 1860)

Twelfth century, English; Calendar, MS Auct. D.2.6., Bodleian. Drawn from The Decorated Letter. J.J.G. Alexander. (Braziller, 1978)

Twentieth century, English. Drawn from postcard.

Fifteenth century, French.
Alphabets & Initials.
(Dover, 1977)   Drawn from Historic
Carol Belanger Grafton.

Tenth century, English or French; Bibliothèque
Municipale, MS 11. Drawn from Medieval Manuscript Painting, Sabrina Mitchell. (Viking, 1964)

Sixteenth century, English. Drawn from a T in Two
Thousand Years of Calligraphy, Baltimore
Museum. (Pentalic, 1980)

Fifteenth century, German. Drawn from Fine
Books, Alan G. Thomas. (Weidenfeld, 1967)

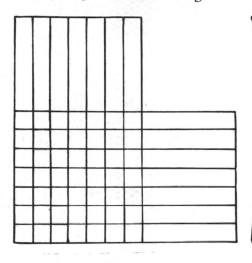

Twentieth century, American, author's design.

Fifteenth century, Italian; Metropolitan Museum of
Art, New York. Drawn from a Christmas card.

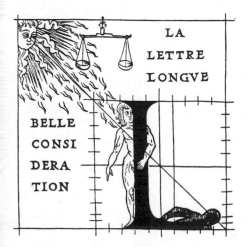

LA
LETTRE
LONGVE

BELLE
CONSI
DERA
TION

Sixteenth century, French; Geofroy Tory. From
Champ Fleury. (Dover, 1967)

Fifteenth century, French. Drawn from Decorative
Alphabets and Initials, Alexander Nesbitt. (Dover,
1959)

Ninth century, Carolingian: The Metz Gospels, ms.
Lat. 9388, Bibliothèque Nationale. Drawn from Letter
and Image, Massin. (Van Nostrand Reinhold, 1970)

Twentieth century, American. Drawn from cover of book by John Cage.

Twentieth century, American. Drawn from an A in The Letter Forms and Type Designs of Eric Gill, Robert Harling. (Godine, 1977)

Fourteenth century, French. Drawn from Historic Alphabets & Initials, Carol Belanger Grafton (Dover, 1977)

Fifteenth century, German. Drawn from Lettering as Ornament, Lewis Day. (Batsford, 1902)

Tenth century, Anglo-Saxon. Drawn from an E in Decorative Alphabets and Initials, Alexander Nesbitt. (Dover, 1959)

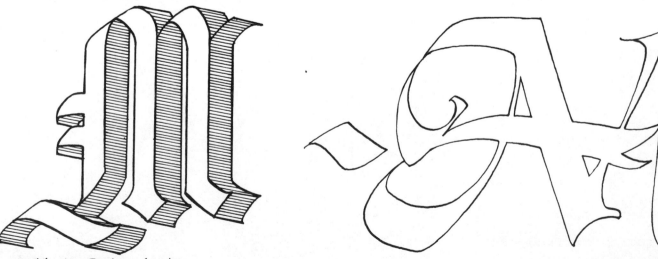

Twentieth century, American, author's design.

Twentieth century, American, author's design.

Eighth century, French. Drawn from The Decorated Letter, J. J. G. Alexander. (Braziller, 1978) Bibliothèque Nationale, Paris.

Fifteenth century, German. Drawn from Five Hundred Years of Printing, S. H. Steinberg. (Penguin, 1974)

Tenth century, German; British Museum, ms. Stowe 3. Drawn from Lettering as Drawing, Nicolete Gray. (Oxford, 1970)

Eighth century, French. Bibliothèque Municipale, Amiens, ms. 18. Drawn from The Decorated Letter, J. J. G. Alexander. (Braziller, 1978)

Eleventh century, German; Walters Art Gallery. Drawn from 2000 Years of Calligraphy, Baltimore Museum of Art. (Pentalic, 1980)

Fourteenth century, German. Drawn from The Art of Illuminating, W. R. Tymms. (Day, 1860)

Sixteenth century, German. From Of the Just Shaping of Letters, Albrecht Dürer. (Dover, 1965)

Fifteenth century, Italian; Metropolitan Museum of Art, New York. Drawn from a Christmas card.

Sixteenth century, Italian. From Alphabets and Initials, Ernst Lehner. (Dover, 1952)

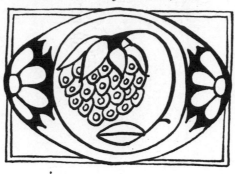

sixteenth century, French. Drawn from Medieval Calligraphy. Marc Drogin. (Schram, 1980)

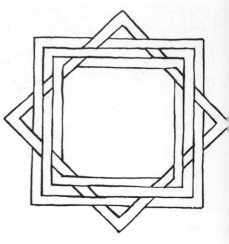

Fifteenth century, German. Drawn from The Art of Illuminating. W.R. Tymms. (Day, 1860)

Twentieth century, American, author's design.

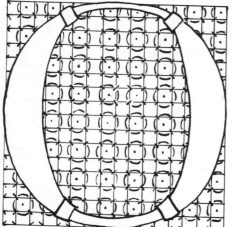

Thirteenth century, German; The Morgan Library, New York. Drawn from The Windmill Psalter.

Sixteenth century, French. Drawn from Historic Alphabets & Initials, Carol Belanger Grafton. (Dover, 1977)

Fourteenth century, French. Drawn from The Art of Illuminating. W.R. Tymms. (Day, 1860)

center: Sixteenth century, French; Geofroy Tory. From Champ Fleury. (Dover, 1967)

Fourteenth century, German. Drawn from The Art of Illuminating. W.R. Tymms. (Day, 1860)

sixteenth century, German. Drawn from Five Hundred Years of Printing. S.H. Steinberg. (Penguin, 1974)

Twentieth century, American, author's design based on a Peruvian tile.

Thirteenth century, French. Drawn from The Art of Illuminating. W. R. Tymms. (Day, 1860)

Sixteenth century, German. Drawn from Historic Alphabets & Initials, Carol Belanger Grafton. (Dover, 1977)

Fifteenth century, French. The Morgan Library, New York. Drawn from The Egmont Breviary.

Nineteenth century, German; Karl Klimsch. Drawn from Florid and Unusual Alphabets. (Dover, 1977)

Fifteenth century, German. From Historic Alphabets & Initials, Carol Belanger Grafton. (Dover, 1977)

Sixteenth century, Italian. Drawn from Five Hundred Years of Printing. S. H. Steinberg. (Penguin, 1974)

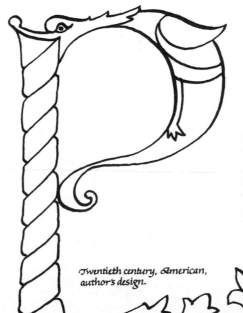

Twentieth century, American, author's design.

Sixteenth century, German. Drawn from Five Hundred Years of Printing, S. H. Steinberg. (Penguin, 1974)

Twentieth century, American, author's design.

Twelfth century, French; The Walters Art Gallery.
Drawn from Two Thousand Years of Calligraphy,
Baltimore Museum. (Pentalic, 1980)

Twentieth century,
American,
author's design

Twentieth century,
American, author's design.

Fifteenth century, German.
Drawn from Five Hundred
Years of Printing, S. H.
Steinberg. (Penguin, 1974)

Sixteenth century, French. Drawn from an O in
The Art of Illuminating, W. R. Tymms.
(Day, 1860)

Twelfth century, French. Drawn from Medieval
Manuscript Painting, Sabrina Mitchell. (Viking
1964)

Tenth century, French. Drawn from The Art of
Illuminating, W. R. Tymms. (Day, 1860)

Fifteenth century, French. Drawn from an A in The Art of Illuminating, W. R. Tymms. (Day, 1860)

Nineteenth century, German; Karl Klimsch. Drawn from Florid and Unusual Alphabets. (Dover, 1976)

Sixteenth century, French; Jean Duvet. Drawn from an A in Alphabets and Ornaments, Ernst Lehner. (Dover, 1952)

Twelfth century, English. Drawn from The Art of Illuminating, W. R. Tymms. (Day, 1860)

Sixteenth century, Spanish; Juan de Yciar. From Alphabets and Ornaments, Ernst Lehner. (Dover, 1952)

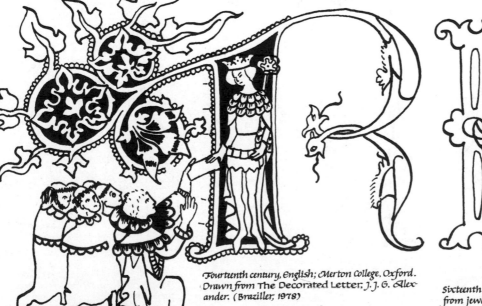

Fourteenth century, English; Merton College, Oxford. Drawn from The Decorated Letter, J. J. G. Alexander. (Braziller, 1978)

Sixteenth century, English; Hans Holbein. Drawn from jewelry and ironwork in Lettering as Ornament, Lewis Day. (Batsford, 1902)

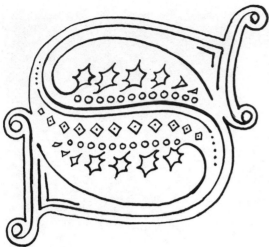

Thirteenth century, Italian. Drawn from The Art of Illuminating, W.R. Tymms. (Day, 1860)

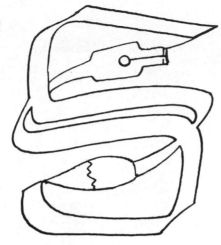

Twentieth century, American, author's design.

Fifteenth century, Italian. Drawn from Decorative Alphabets and Initials, Alexander Nesbitt. (Dover, 1959)

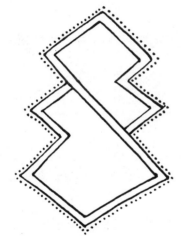

Eighth century, Irish. Drawn from The Book of Kells. (Knopf, 1974)

Nineteenth century, German; Karl Klimsch. From Florid and Unusual Alphabets. (Dover, 1976)

Sixteenth century, French; Jean Duvet. Drawn from Alphabets and Ornaments, Ernst Lehner. (Dover, 1952)

Fourteenth century, English. Drawn from Decorative Alphabets and Initials, Alexander Nesbitt. (Dover, 1959)

Fourteenth century, Italian. Drawn from The Art of Illuminating, W.R. Tymms. (Day, 1860)

Sixteenth century, Peruvian; Antonio Ricardo, printer. Drawn from "First Printings of South America in the Harvard Library," Antonio Rodriguez. Harvard Library Bulletin, Volume XVI, #1, January 1968.

Nineteenth century, English. Drawn from an L in Writing and Illuminating and Lettering, Edward Johnston. (Pentalic, 1979)

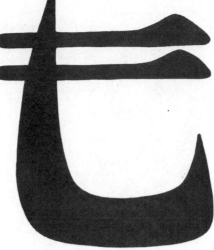

Twentieth century, American. From Special-effects and Topical Alphabets, Dan X. Solo. (Dover, 1978)

Fifteenth century, Italian. Drawn from Suggestions for Illuminating, W. Randle Harrison. (Vincent, 1907)

Twentieth century, American. Drawn from an O and a T in Special-effects and Topical Alphabets, Dan X. Solo. (Dover, 1978)

Twelfth century, French? From Decorative Alphabets and Initials, Alexander Nesbitt. (Dover, 1959)

Fifteenth century, German. Drawn from Historic Alphabets & Initials, Carol Belanger Grafton. (Dover, 1977)

Twentieth century, American. From an illustration in the Book Review of the Sunday New York Times.

Nineteenth century, English; William Morris. Drawn from Five Hundred Years of Printing, S. H. Steinberg. (Penguin, 1974)

Fourteenth century, Italian. Drawn from The Visconti Hours. (Braziller, 1972)

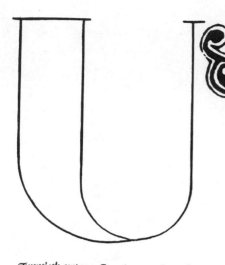

Twentieth century, American, author's design.

Fifteenth century, German. From The Art of Illuminating, W. R. Tymms. (Day, 1860)

Fourteenth century, Italian. Drawn from The Visconti Hours. (Braziller, 1972)

Nineteenth century, French; Silvestre. From Florid and Unusual Alphabets. (Dover, 1976)

Fifteenth century, French. Drawn from Two Thousand Years of Calligraphy, Baltimore Museum. (Pentalic, 1980)

Nineteenth century, French; Silvestre. From Florid and Unusual Alphabets. (Dover, 1976)

Fourteenth century, Italian. Drawn from The Visconti Hours. (Braziller, 1972)

Eighth century, French; Library of France #626. Drawn from The Art of Illuminating. W. R. Tymms. (Day, 1860)

Fifteenth century, German. Drawn from Decorative Alphabets and Initials, Alexander Nesbitt. (Dover, 1959)

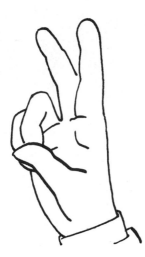

Nineteenth century, American. Drawn from manual alphabet for the deaf.

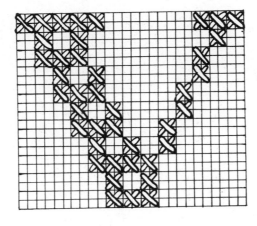

Nineteenth century, English. Drawn from cross-stitch sampler by Mary Keachie, author's collection.

Twentieth century, American; author's design.

Sixteenth century, French. From Five Hundred Years of Printing, S.H. Steinberg (Penguin, 1974)

Eleventh century, Italian. Drawn from Medieval Manuscript Painting, Sabrina Mitchell. (Viking, 1964)

Fifteenth century, Italian? Drawn from The Art of Illuminating, W.R. Tymms. (Day, 1860)

Eighth century, Irish. Drawn from The Book of Kells. (Knopf, 1974)

Fifteenth century, Italian; Perotti's translation of Poly-bius, ex Libris H. Yates Thompson. Drawn from an A in Writing and Illuminating and Lettering, Edward Johnston. (Pentalic, 1979)

Eighth century, Irish. Drawn from Th Kells. (Knopf, 1974)

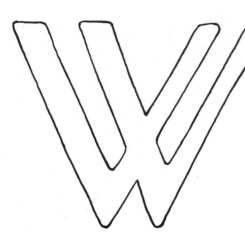

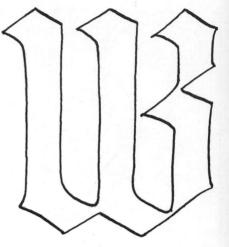

Twentieth century, American. Drawn from The New Yorker magazine.

Fifteenth century, Flemish. Drawn from an M in Two Thousand Years of Calligraphy, Baltimore Museum. (Pentalic, 1980)

Fifteenth century, German. Drawn from Historic Alphabets & Initials, Carol Belanger Grafton. (Dover, 1977)

Fifteenth century, Dutch. Drawn from an M in Two Thousand Years of Calligraphy, Baltimore Museum. (Pentalic, 1980)

Twentieth century, American. From an alphabet in New York Magazine by Robert Grossman.

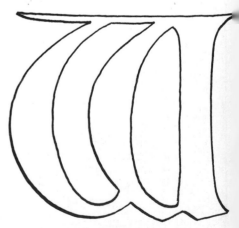

Twentieth century, American; author's design.

Nineteenth century, English; William Morris. Drawn from The Kelmscott Chaucer.

Nineteenth century, German; Karl Klimsch. From Florid and Unusual Alphabets. (Dover, 1976)

Nineteenth century, German. Drawn from Historic
Alphabets & Initials, Carol Belanger Grafton.
(Dover, 1977)

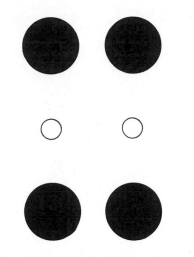

Nineteenth century, French; Louis Braille. Drawn
from raised alphabet for the blind.

Fourteenth century, Italian. Drawn from The
Visconti Hours. (Braziller, 1972)

Seventeenth century, Italian. From Historic
Alphabets & Initials, Carol Belanger Grafton.
(Dover, 1977)

Fourteenth century, Italian. Drawn from The
Visconti Hours. (Braziller, 1972)

Twentieth century, American, author's design.

Eighth century, Irish. Drawn from a knot in
The Book of Kells. (Knopf, 1974)

Twentieth century, American; author's design.

Fifteenth century, German. Drawn from Decorative Alphabets and Initials, Alexander
Nesbitt. (Dover, 1959)

Nineteenth century, French; Silvestre. From Florid and Unusual Alphabets. (Dover, 1976)

Fifteenth century, German. Drawn from The Art of Illuminating, W.R.Tymms. (Day, 1860)

Twentieth century German. From Historic Alphabets & Initials, Carol Belanger Grafton. (Dover, 1977)

Fifteenth century, German. Drawn from Decorative Alphabets and Initials, Alexander Nesbitt. (Dover, 1959)

Sixteenth century, French; Geofroy Tory. From Champ Fleury. (Dover, 1967)

Fifteenth century, German. Drawn from The Art of Illuminating, W.R.Tymms. (Day, 1860)

Sixteenth century, French; Geofroy Tory. From Champ Fleury. (Dover, 1967)

Fifteenth century, German. Drawn from Decorative Alphabets and Initials, Alexander Nesbitt. (Dover, 1959)

Twentieth century, American. Drawn from The ABC Bunny, Wanda Gag. (Coward McCann, 1933)

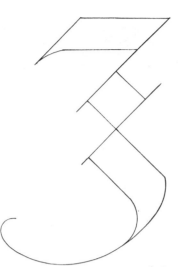

Twentieth century, American; author's design.

Twentieth century, American; author's design.

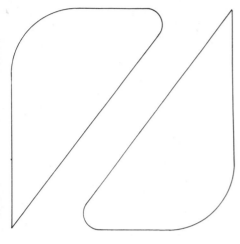

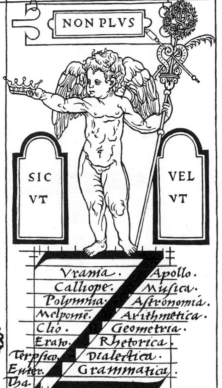

Twentieth century, American; author's design.

Sixteenth century, French; Geofroy Tory. From Champ Fleury. (Dover, 1967)

Nineteenth century, German. From Decorative Alphabets and Initials, Alexander Nesbitt. (Dover, 1959)

Eleventh century, French or Spanish. Drawn from an N in Medieval Calligraphy, Marc Drogin. (Schram, 1980)

Twentieth century, German; Jan Tschichold. From Jan Tschichold: Typographer. (Godine, 1975)

Twentieth century, American; author's design.

BIBLIOGRAPHY

GLOSSARY AND INDEX

BIBLIOGRAPHY

Alexander, J.J.G., The Decorated Letter. New York: George
    Braziller, 1978.

Alphabets, Monograms, Initials, Crests, etc. New York:
    E. W. Bullinger, c. 1890.

Anderson, Donald, The Art of Written Forms. New York:
    Holt, Rinehart and Winston, 1969.

Angel, Marie, An Animated Alphabet. Cambridge, Mass.:
    Harvard College Library, Department of Printing and
    Graphic Arts, 1971.

Angel, Marie, The Art of Calligraphy: A Practical Guide.
    New York: Charles Scribner's Sons, 1977.

Angel, Marie, A New Bestiary. Cambridge, Mass.: Harvard
    College Library, Department of Printing and Graphic
    Arts, 1964.

Astle, Thomas, The Origin and Progress of Writing.
    London: J. White, 1803.

Backhouse, Janet, The Illuminated Manuscript. Oxford:
    Phaidon, 1979.

Bain, George, Celtic Art: The Methods of Construction.
    New York: Dover, 1975.

Baker, Arthur, Arthur Baker's Historic Calligraphic Alphabets. New York: Dover, 1980.

Baker, Arthur, Dance of the Pen. New York: Art Direction Book Company, 1978.

Baltimore Museum, Two Thousand Years of Calligraphy. New York: Pentalic, 1980.

The Belles Heures of Jean, Duke of Berry. New York: George Braziller, 1974.

Bland, David, A History of Book Illustration: The Illuminated Manuscript and The Printed Book. Berkeley: University of California Press, 1969.

Blumenthal, Joseph, Art of the Printed Book, 1455-1955. Boston: David R. Godine, 1973.

Bodleian Library, Oxford University, Humanistic Script of the Fifteenth and Sixteenth Centuries. Oxford: Bodleian, 1960.

The Book of Kells. New York: Alfred A. Knopf, 1974.

Butsch, Albert Fidelis, Handbook of Renaissance Ornament. New York: Dover, 1969.

Child, Heather, Calligraphy Today. New York: Pentalic, 1976.

Cresci, Giovan Francesco, A Renaissance Alphabet. Madison, Wis.: University of Wisconsin Press, 1971.

Day, Lewis F., Alphabets Old and New. London: Charles Scribner's Sons, 1902.

Day, Lewis F., Lettering in Ornament. London: Batsford, 1902.

Degering, Hermann, Lettering. New York: Pentalic, 1965.

Drogin, Marc, Medieval Calligraphy. Montclair, N.J.: Abner Schram, 1980.

Dürer, Albrecht, Of the Just Shaping of Letters. New York: Dover, 1965.

Gillon, Edmund V., ed., Pictorial Calligraphy and Ornamentation. New York: Dover, 1972.

Goudy, Frederic W., The Alphabet and Elements of Lettering. New York: Dover, 1977.

Gourdie, Tom, Calligraphic Styles. New York: Pentalic, 1979.

Grafton, Carol Belanger, Historic Alphabets, Woodcut and Ornamental. New York: Dover, 1977.

Gray, Nicolete, Lettering as Drawing: The Moving Line. London: Oxford University Press, 1970.

Gray, Nicolete, Lettering as Drawing: Contour and Silhouette. London: Oxford University Press, 1970.

Harling, Robert, ed., The Letter Forms and Type Designs of Eric Gill. Boston: David R. Godine, 1977.

Harvard College Library, Illuminated and Calligraphic Manuscripts. Cambridge, Mass.: Harvard College Library, Department of Printing and Graphic Arts, 1955.

The Hours of Catherine of Cleves. New York: George Braziller, 1975.

Hyde, Robert C., A Dictionary for Calligraphers. Los Angeles: Martin Press, 1977.

Jackson, Donald, The Story of Writing. New York: Taplinger, 1981.

Johnson, A.F., Decorative Alphabets and Initials. London: Cresset Press, 1931.

Johnston, Edward, Writing and Illuminating and Lettering. New York: Pentalic, 1975.

Koch, Rudolf, and Berthold Wolpe, The Little ABC Book of Rudolf Koch. Boston: David R. Godine, 1976.

Larcher, Jean, Fantastic Alphabets. New York: Dover, 1976.

Lehner, Ernst, Alphabets and Ornaments. New York: Dover, 1952.

Loeb, Marcia, New Art Deco Alphabets. New York: Dover, 1975.

Macdonald, Byron J., Calligraphy: The Art of Lettering with the Broad Pen. New York: Pentalic, 1978.

McLean, Rauri, Jan Tschichold: Typographer. Boston: David R. Godine, 1975.

Menton, Theodore, ed., Art Nouveau and Early Art Deco Type and Design. New York: Dover, 1978.

Midolle, Silvestre, et al., Florid and Unusual Alphabets. New York: Dover, 1976.

Mitchell, Sabrina, Medieval Manuscript Painting. New York: Viking, 1964.

Modern Scribes and Lettering Artists. New York: Pentalic, 1980.

Munch, Gary J., Hand-to-Hand Combat: The Struggle for Supremacy of Scripts Developed in the Renaissance. Eugene, Ore.: Instant Incunable Imprimatur, 1980.

Nesbitt, Alexander, Decorative Alphabets and Initials. New York: Dover, 1957.

Ogg, Oscar, ed., Three Classics of Italian Calligraphy: An Unabridged Reissue of the Writing Books of Arrighi, Tagliente, and Palatino. New York: Dover, 1953.

Rodriguez-Buckingham, Antonio, "First Printings of South America in the Harvard Library." Harvard Library Bulletin, volume 16, no. 1. Cambridge, Mass.: Harvard University Press, 1968.

Shahn, Ben, Love and Joy About Letters. New York: Crossman Publishers, 1963.

Solo, Dan, Special-effects and Topical Alphabets. New York: Dover, 1978.

Steinberg, S.H., Five Hundred Years of Printing. New York: Penguin, 1969.

Strange, Edward F., Alphabets: A Manual of Lettering for Use of Students, with Historical and Practical Descriptions. London: G. Bell and Sons, 1921.

Svaren, Jacqueline, Written Letters: 22 Alphabets for Calligraphers. Freeport, Me.: Bond Wheelwright, 1975.

Sweeney, James Johnson, ed., Irish Illuminated Manuscripts of the Early Christian Period. New York: New American Library, 1965.

Thomas, Alan G., Fine Books. London: Weidenfeld and
        Nicolson, 1967.

Tory, Geofroy, Champ Fleury. New York: Dover, 1967.

Treasures of Early Irish Art. New York: Metropolitan
        Museum of Art, 1977.

Tymms, W. R., ed., The Art of Illuminating as Practiced
        in Europe from the Earliest Times. London:
        Day and Son, 1860

The Visconti Hours. New York: George Braziller, 1972.

GLOSSARY AND INDEX

Page numbers refer to main sections dealing with the defined term. Un-numbered words are not dealt with in the text but may help enrich the reader's understanding and rendering of the capital letters that are illustrated in this book.

81   ABECEDARY. An alphabetical collection or compilation, often of diverse objects or ideas.

15   ASCENDER. The part of a small letter that extends above its body. See DESCENDER.

57   AXIS OF SYMMETRY. The imaginary line that divides a symmetrical letter or stroke into two mirror-image halves.

ascender · *if* · *Descender*

BLACKLETTER. A rendering of the Gothic letter where spaces inside or between letters are narrower than the width of the letter stroke itself.

CAPITAL. A letterform distinguished from its related SMALL LETTER by size and shape, and used in place of the small letter for linguistic or decorative reasons, or both. The relationship between capital and small letter is expressed in the Latin terms MAJUSCULE and MINUSCULE, and in the typographic terms UPPER CASE and LOWER CASE. See INITIAL.

to **to**
Gothic Blackletter

69   CAROLINGIAN. A ninth-century small-letter style,

redesigned by Charlemagne's scribes from sixth-century half-uncials. Precursor of Renaissance BOOKHAND.

15, 30   CELTIC. A seventh-century uncial letter style, related to Roman capitals but distinguished by Irish serif and shape, and flexible use as capital & text letter.

48   CLASSIC or Old Style. A typographic term, designating a Roman capital style that imitates the curves and proportions of the handlettered original, in contrast to the MODERN style, which relies on geometry.

30   COMMONCASE. A typographic term describing the intermixing of upper- and lower-case letters.

10-11   CROWQUILL. Originally a sharp feather pen, now a sharp metal pen.

15   DESCENDER. See ASCENDER.

7-9   FELT PEN. A plastic or metal pen with a wick-like, non-removable rigid fiber nib impregnated with a non-renewable ink supply.

FINIAL. See INITIAL.

5-6   FOUNTAIN PEN. A plastic or metal pen with a flexible ink reservoir and a metal nib.

60   FOLIATION. Decoration of a capital with leaves & flowers.

26   GREEK. Precursor of ROMAN.

16-17   GOTHIC. Angular medieval letter.

HISTORIATION. Decoration of a capital with scenes depicting a specific tale or a real event.

ILLUMINATION. Decoration of a capital with gold leaf. Also used to describe ornamentation in general.

12 INDIA INK. Waterproof black writing fluid made of a suspension of finely ground carbon particles.

INITIAL. First letter in a word or on a page. A middle letter is MEDIAL, and a letter at the end is FINIAL.

LETTER BODY. Main part of small letter, excluding ascenders and descenders. Can be called a 'counter,' although this is usually limited to the white space enclosed within some letter bodies.

LOWER CASE. A typographic term meaning small or minuscule letter, derived from the relative placement of the flat boxes full of the various letters that a type compositor used to set type. See LOWER CASE.

MAJUSCULE. Capital letter. See CAPITAL.

MEDIAL. See INITIAL.

MINIATURE. Small, detailed illumination or book illustration. Originally done quickly in red lead paint (minium), these pictures became a highly detailed art.

MINUSCULE. Small letter. See CAPITAL.

48 MODERN. An eighteenth-century typographic term describing a Roman capital style. See CLASSIC.

NIB. Pen point. See FELT PEN, FOUNTAIN PEN.

2 QUILL. Strong wing feather of a goose or swan.

RESERVOIR. Container for storing ink behind or under the pen nib, to minimize necessity to refill pen.

50 ROCOCO. An eighteenth-century decorative style, characterized by restless, asymmetrical curves.

28　ROMAN. Classic capital letter, ancestor of nearly all
　　Western letters.

60　TROMPE L'OEIL. A kind of painting done with the
　　intent of creating a three-dimensional illusion of
　　depth. Literally 'a trick to the eye.'

This book was written out in a plain Italic letter style 1½
times larger than final size, on Strathmore Calligraphy
Document paper using a Koh-I-Noor Calligraphy
pen (Broad nib) custom-designed for the author.
The drawings were done with a Koh-I-Noor
Artpen; the headings and alphabets
were done with a Mitchell
Roundhand pen. Liquid
Paper covered all
mistakes or
nearly
all
·